FUTUREHACK!

HOW TO REACH YOUR
FULL FINANCIAL POTENTIAL

READY TO #FUTUREHACK YOUR LIFE?

I've put together a FREE training revealing:

- The Invst4Life process to help you live the life you want

- The 4 challenges to building wealth

- And proven strategies to make money work for you

Are you ready to invest in you, your family, and your future AND improve your cash flow to protect your value and reach your full financial potential?

Head over to **www.futurehackmylife.com** to access this free training now!

FUTUREHACK!

HOW TO REACH YOUR
FULL FINANCIAL POTENTIAL

SCOTT JARRED

Printed in the United States of America.
Library of Congress Control Number: 2020919932
ISBN Casebound: 978-1-7351112-0-9
ISBN Paperback: 978-1-9496396-1-2
Cover Design: Carly Blake
Layout Design: Mary Hamilton

I want to dedicate this book not only to those people whom I have learned from but also to those whom they learned from. This book is a collection of all those ideas, truths, and actions that have been paid forward. I truly believe this knowledge is what allows us to hack our future to live the life we want.

CONTENTS

INTRODUCTION 1

HOW TO MAKE YOUR FINANCIAL LIFE RADICALLY BETTER

CHAPTER ONE 15

BE AN ABUNDANT THINKER

CHAPTER TWO 33

ALWAYS EVOLVE

CHAPTER THREE 45

HATERS GONNA HATE—SO BEAT 'EM AT THEIR OWN GAME

CHAPTER FOUR 57

ADAPT TO CHANGE

CHAPTER FIVE 75

CONTROL YOUR CONTROLLABLES— PROTECT YOURSELF!

CHAPTER SIX 89
BE A WORLD-CLASS SAVER

CHAPTER SEVEN 103
LIVE YOUR LIFE—AND INSURE IT RIGHT

CHAPTER EIGHT 121
BUILD YOUR GAME BOARD

CHAPTER NINE 135
**CREATE AN EVIDENCE-BASED INVESTMENT
PHILOSOPHY THAT WORKS FOR YOU**

CHAPTER TEN 147
GET SOME MOMENTUM WITH FACTOR VI

CONCLUSION 165
IT'S TIME TO #FUTUREHACK!

APPENDIX 171
INTERACTIVE FUTURE HACKS

HOW TO MAKE YOUR FINANCIAL LIFE RADICALLY BETTER

I f you were to write your obituary right now, what would it say? Seriously, have you thought about the dash between when you were born and when you will die? This may seem morbid. But it clearly distills what you want to be remembered about your life. About who you want to be. About what you want to accomplish. About the legacy you want to leave behind. If you don't understand what you *want* in and from your life, then you can't work to achieve it.

Beyond this critical foundation is the ability to fuel your life— money. Too many of us struggle with anxiety over money. Income, debt, career, lifestyle, taxes, and so much more put pressure on your dollars. Anxiety leads to poor decisions, poor health, strained relationships, and distraction from what you really want for your life.

I've been there.

The good news is you don't have to be there. And if you're not quite that bad, there is still great room for growth and an even more rewarding life.

> # Traditional thinking has limited your potential for too long.

Traditional thinking has limited your potential for too long. I escaped the anxiety-ridden life to create the life I want, to define my "dash" myself. The purpose of creating my firm, JarredBunch Consulting, is to help people achieve their goals, their dreams, their wants, the *life* they want to live.

It All Begins with the Right Mindset

With the right mindset, you can accomplish more on your own than you've ever imagined. It's time to live the life you want to live, to make your financial life radically better, to unleash your full potential, to change your tomorrow by hacking your future today.

I've always been an entrepreneur. In fact, I've never really had a choice but to be an entrepreneur. I didn't have much when I was a kid. I grew up in a low-income family with a single mother, living in subsidized housing and relying on food stamps. We were fighting just to survive.

That fight motivated me, from a very young age, to figure out how to make opportunities happen for myself. At age twelve, I had a paper route, and before long, I had expanded and taken over the whole neighborhood. I even had people working for me. When I was in high school, I started playing football, and I had a carpet-cleaning business that helped get me through high school. Luckily, I was able to get a full-ride scholarship to college to play football. College wasn't really for my family or for people like me. No one in my family had ever gone before. When we were asked in high school who was going to college, I didn't even raise my hand, because I didn't think it was an option. Football was my way out; it was a chance to see the world, and I jumped on that train. My first year in college was rough as I had no idea what to study. I was only academically eligible because of the special NCAA standards for athletes. My guidance counselor thought it would be best to pick an easy major so I could stay in. So I chose criminal justice.

In one of my first classes, I had to interview professionals, and I met a computer-aided design specialist who was designing a building for a local real estate developer. In talking to him, I decided that being a real estate developer was my ticket and I had to find a college offering that program. I found a program at Ball State University in Indiana, so I transferred immediately.

I finished college, maximizing every credit hour I could get, from economics to entrepreneurship, architecture to urban planning. I really wanted to be a real estate developer—that's where the money was, and it looked fun. When I first got to Ball State, I walked straight into the College of Architecture and Planning and asked the front secretary, "How do I get into this program?" She gave me a look before she answered and said, "We are a top ranked college, and most of our students are presidential scholars. What have you done?" I certainly wasn't a presidential scholar, but I wasn't deterred. I asked her who makes admission decisions and if I could I have their phone number. Long story short: I brought my C average up, and I got in. But when I eventually graduated, I didn't have any money to get started as an actual developer, so I went back to school and earned my master's in technology. I had friends who were out of school and making bank in the technology industry. I figured I would be able to build tele-communication facilities, which was the highest price-per-foot in real estate. It wasn't long before I landed a corporate job with a high-tech company and moved from Indianapolis, Indiana, to Tampa, Florida. I was making great money. I had, by any measure, "made it."

Next Ten Years?

But once I was there, I started asking myself, "Now what? Where will I be ten years from now?" I realized that just "making it" wasn't enough; I wanted to do something more. I wanted to help people and not corporations. I really wanted to make a difference in people's lives, and I wanted to help them achieve financial stability, indepen-dence, and control over their financial futures. That's all I wanted for myself, and I thought others had the same issue.

When I left Indianapolis and moved to Tampa, I moved into a three-bedroom apartment overlooking the water with two other roommates. One of them, Branden Bunch, worked in financial services and happened to have a big TV and great living room furniture. He was a perfect roommate for a couple of guys right out of college. One day when we were talking about what the future could hold, I said to Branden, "Hey, let's start a consulting company for small-business owners that helps people with their money." So Branden quit his job, and we split my paycheck while we focused on getting the business up and running. Once we had enough clients, I left corporate America for good—and in 2003, JarredBunch Con-sulting was born.

All I knew at the time was that JarredBunch was created to help business owners. Owners needed help with employer-sponsored benefits. It quickly became apparent there were several other needs as well. Mainly, the owners themselves needed personal financial help. They were good businesspeople but very poor at managing their personal financial lives.

The easiest path to start was also a traditional path. The financial industry, at the time, had very few independent firms. Most were affiliated with broker-dealers. That traditional path gave us a start, but it limited what we could do for our clients. Not only in coaching and consulting but also in how we provided planning, investment management, and other services. The goal of the broker-dealer is to sell products. We were registered representatives of ... salespeople for their products. This became unacceptable for us.

Once the goals of the institutions became apparent (more on this later in this book), I knew JarredBunch had to leave the traditional model. I wanted to sit on the same side of the table as our clients, to offer what I believed was in *their* best interests not the best interests of the institution.

So began the next leg of my journey.

I abandoned a pension, renewal income, and the perceived "safety" of the traditional financial industry to create something bigger than myself. As an SEC-registered investment advisory firm, I was now forever free to tell the real financial story and to completely implement financial strategies that would radically help the clients we serve as a true fiduciary.

Mission Driven

Our mission statement is, and always has been, to help educate, counsel, and guide our clients toward reaching their full financial potential. Whether you are a business owner, a corporate employee, or someone starting up your own business, JarredBunch was built to help you create a radically better financial future for yourself and your family.

Doing that demands following a strategy—and even fiduciaries don't necessarily adhere to a comprehensive, rules-based, wealth-building strategy. That's why it's important to create one for yourself. If you can write your own story and dream what you want yourself, then you won't be submitting to someone else's agenda, one which may not be in your best interest. You decide what you want, and then you go and find the solution that achieves your bigger future.

Rules to the Game

Any pension plan, any endowment, any large family office will have what's called an investment policy statement. Your IPS lays out the rules for how the money is supposed to be managed. How your money supports your life. We believe that everyone should have an understanding of—and a say in—how their money is managed. There should be some form of evidence and rules behind every financial decision that fits with that person's "Investor DNA." Your Investor DNA is unique to you. It's how you are wired to use, live with, and invest your money. Understanding this is a critical component of your financial life success.

Certain people have been mind-blowingly successful at managing their money; some have even won Nobel Prizes for their proven financial strategies: Warren Buffett, Eugene Fama, Kenneth French, and Ray Dalio, for example. What's their secret? They each developed a strategy, a set of principles and rules, and adhered to it. These strategies are defined and are backed by a rules-based philosophy that adheres to their personal Investor DNA. Each of these individuals used a form of evidence to complete their philosophy, and their wild success proves their strategies really work.

We know what doesn't work: speculation, stock picking, market timing—it's all gambling. Instead of gambling, you should be using a strategy that focuses on the risk of loss first, that will adhere to the sequence-of-return risk, and that you can stick with for the long haul.

Why? Because human beings are by nature irrational. We live lives of uncertainty. As much as we might try to be logical, we are not robots. We have emotions, and those emotions influence our actions, for better or for worse. We often act out of fear. We get sick; we're mortal; we worry about illness, about dying too young, about outliving our means. We want to make sure our loved ones are taken care of. We worry about whether the market is too high or too low, whether we need to get out or stay in. But if you can find a strategy that works for you, you can abide by those rules. Rules allow you to stick with a system, rather than being emotional, illogical, or impulsive about your investment decisions.

Of course, past performance is no indication of future performance. You have to take into account risks and volatility and how those strategies will react to a changing world and the unknowns of the future. The world is always evolving—and today, it's changing faster than ever. Back in the 1970s, the Greatest Generation had gold backing their money. It was a totally different time, which you can hardly compare to where we are right now. But people are still planning their finances in the same old way. What our grandparents did wasn't bad by any means—they were the Greatest Generation after all—but things are different now.

New Economy

Thirty years ago, people worked their whole career at one company and retired with defined pension plans. That's hardly ever the case today. People change careers and jobs all the time, usually without a pension; instead, they piece together a living in the gig economy, creating their own little microeconomies. The traditional financial institutional structures often don't apply.

Most of the wealth in the world today is controlled by the top 1 percent. What are they doing to hold on to that wealth? What were the traditions that worked for the tycoons and icons in the past that was lost upon the rest of the world, and what can we learn from them? How can the rest of us do the same in a system that has its own agenda? And how do we turn that agenda around to work in our favor?

To survive and flourish, you have to adapt and evolve. How can you build strategies and financial plans that ride the momentum of current trends, that evolve as the world does, that adapt to the changes—both expected and unexpected—that happen in your life?

Just Hack It

By hacking the system. By not following blindly, but instead becoming the author of your own plan. It's time to create a system that works for you. It's time to hack your financial future, to reach your full financial potential, to become work optional and financially independent while making your financial life radically better.

* * *

What does making your financial life radically better look like? What does it look like to reach your full financial potential? It's not about just making as much money as you possibly can. It's what you can *do* with your money that counts—and that goes far beyond just self-serving wealth accumulation.

I recall asking one of our ultrahigh-net–worth clients, who is now in his seventies, about his future plans. This client has been extremely successful—and yet he still wanted to keep growing his wealth. "Do you really need to go through all the trouble to develop another hotel?" I asked him. "Do you really need to take this business to the next level?"

"Yeah," he said to me. "Why not?"

So we started talking, and I learned that what he really wanted was to give back to society. He had arrived in the US on a boat from another country, and he was trying to save people back in his homeland. He had made a fortune, and he realized that his potential to help others was endless. He used the hotel development project to hire hundreds of people using the EB-5 Immigrant Investor Program, which allowed investors to fund the project and bring people from his homeland to America.

Everyone wants to do something different with his or her money, so hitting your full financial potential is going to look very different for each person. Warren Buffett and Bill Gates are huge philanthropists. Once they amassed their fortunes, they decided they wanted to help millions more people. Some people want to live a lavish lifestyle. Some people are happy with very little, living in a small house with their spouse and kids. One of our clients has a billion dollars in real estate, but he doesn't own a car. That's just not important to him, but urban culture and revitalization are. Some people want to retire and be able to live comfortably off what they've saved; others want to keep working, to evolve their business and leave a legacy.

To hack your future, you have to unlock your mind. Reaching

your full financial potential means reaching your full life potential. If you don't unlock your mind to see the possibilities, you can't create a financial plan to reach your full potential. In order to do that, you have to think abundantly. Personal finance has to be *personal,* and you are the greatest asset. Oftentimes financial transactions do not take that into consideration and become a distraction and limitation rather than enhancing wealth around you.

I always thought that as soon as my wealth grew to where I didn't have to work anymore, I'd be done. But I reached that point sooner than I anticipated, and I wasn't ready to walk away. So my potential shifted. I realized that I had the potential to make things better for people, to transform the financial industry. Even better, I had the potential to create a life where I could do that, have fun doing it, and still get to spend as much time with my family as I wanted.

IT'S NOT ABOUT MONEY

Reaching your full financial potential isn't really about the money. It's about achieving your dreams. It's about living the life you want to live. The money is just what allows you to do what you want to do.

> **Your financial life is the fuel for the rest of your life.**

Your financial life is the fuel for the rest of your life. You can't make financial decisions in a vacuum. Every financial choice has a butterfly effect. If you throw a rock into a pond, you see the splash it makes—but the rock does more than just splash. It also causes ripples that extend out through the water and affect the whole pond.

A financial decision is the same: its ripples extend out and affect your whole life. You can't just pay attention to the splash; you have to pay attention to the ripples as well. Every financial decision you make—whether it's putting money in a 401(k) or a 529 college savings plan; paying off your house; paying off your car; buying life insurance, car insurance, or homeowner's insurance; quitting your job; or investing in a business—has repercussions.

Looking at financial decisions in a vacuum is like going to a specialist and saying, "My shoulder hurts," and the doctor saying, "Great, let's operate," without considering the rest of your body. Perhaps the hurt shoulder is just a symptom of a greater problem, like a pending heart attack, which should be addressed first. And yet, many financial advisors do operate in a vacuum. Why? Because we live in a specialist society. Everybody specializes in something—one specific part of the body—and the bigger picture gets missed.

I created JarredBunch because I wanted to look at the whole of someone's financial life, not just a part. The only way to make truly informed financial decisions is to have everything organized, to see the big picture of your entire financial world. That's a lot of information, a lot of chess pieces that need to be managed. How do you deal with all those pieces?

Well, you can't play chess without a chessboard. You can have all the pieces, but if you don't have a board to put them on, you can't play the game. To put all your financial pieces on the same game board, you need to break down the evidenced-based principles and rules that you are going to play by—and stick to them. Just as you do with chess, you have to plan several moves ahead. Without a forward-planning process, you're playing checkers, not chess. When you apply your rules to your financial life, you're now playing chess and have a higher likelihood of success.

One big problem is getting chess pieces to work together for the common goal. This is called compartmentalizing. On average you interact with thirteen financial institutions. Plus you've got your investment guy, your car insurance guy, your mortgage broker, your banker, your life insurance salesperson, your CPA, your attorney. When's the last time all those people were actually in the same room creating a comprehensive plan for your financial future? And often, even if those people do get together, things still get all mixed up. Why? Because there is no overall game plan. There are no rules. There are no overarching strategies or philosophies.

This is how things work, even at the highest level. Successful families have family offices, investment policy statements, a protection strategy, and a healthy balance sheet. Unsuccessful families very rarely put all those things together, coordinate them, or organize them. Rather than playing a strategic chess game, they are playing seven or eight different games all at the same time. When you set core principles and rules to follow, then all those disparate pieces start working together to achieve the same objective: unlocking your full financial potential.

The Ten Components

In this book, we'll explore ten components that will help you set those rules and principles for yourself. Now, in one place you have the sum total of our experience—all the things we've learned—to break down this financial journey into something that's simple and manageable. Your plan—your financial model—will set you on the path to personal financial independence.

Although every person's financial situation is unique, we believe certain philosophies, principles, rules, and mindsets are common across the board. Whether you are within corporate America and trying to work your way out, like I was, or you're in corporate America and trying to grow within or you're a business owner trying to scale for the next generation or trying to sell—whatever your situation, these ten steps will help you reach your full financial potential.

Ultimately, it's not our financial plan. It's yours. We want to give you the structure to start that conversation, the foundation on which to build. This book is a road map—ten steps, based on our expertise and everything we've learned—so you, too, can hack your future to live the life you really want to live. As you continue to read, we will identify the "hack" (a simple solution to a common problem) of living the life you want to live and reaching financial independence. These ten steps will give you more protection, set your own agenda, find lost money, improve your cash flow, and help you define rules for your money.

Are you ready to #FutureHack your financial life? Head over to www.futurehackmylife.com to get started!

CHAPTER ONE

BE AN ABUNDANT THINKER

Growing up, I had the pleasure of living in subsidized housing—and it was the best learning experience of my life (although it sure didn't feel like it at the time). Why? Because I experienced firsthand the insidious power of the scarcity mindset, and eventually, I learned how to pull myself out of it and into a mindset of abundance.

Two Kinds of People

Over my years of working with clients, I've found that all people fall into one of these two mindsets: those who live in abundance, and those who live in a world of scarcity. What is scarcity? In the 1950s, psychologist Abraham Maslow proposed a theory that has become known as Maslow's hierarchy of needs. The baseline of the hierarchy of human need is physiological: food, water, shelter—the minimum requirements for the human body to survive. Merriam-Webster defines scarcity as "the quality or state of being scarce; especially: want of provisions for the support of life"—i.e., the elements found at the baseline of Maslow's hierarchy. When you live in a situation in which that minimum baseline necessary for survival is not a sure thing, or you think it's not a sure thing, it's all you can focus on. All you are thinking about is what you can get your hands on just to get by.

This is exactly what I experienced growing up in subsidized housing: scarcity at its height. Everywhere I turned, I was surrounded by people with scarcity mindsets, or worse, poverty mindsets. Excuses were plentiful. But a lack of thinking beyond today, the moment, was how I was raised. I heard every excuse you can think of: "I can't get that job." "If I make too much money, the welfare checks will stop coming." When you're surrounded by that kind of thinking, it can be very hard to pull yourself out. That negative vibe is real and contagious—and usually, it's completely unconscious. Many people don't realize they have a scarcity mindset because it is so deeply ingrained. It may even be comfortable. That's what I saw—and what I felt—growing up.

With a scarcity mindset, you get stuck in your current situation. You can't see the bigger picture. You can't imagine a future that looks different from your present. You can't fathom future possibilities. When I was growing up, it was always difficult for us just to get by. When you're struggling to pay the bills, the idea of leaving the neighborhood and getting a well-paying job seems completely outside the realm of possibility.

But it's not just about getting stuck in the neighborhood or situation you grew up in. A scarcity-minded person is one who stays in an unhappy position, such as the same job or the same company, for years, even decades, for fear of losing out on good benefits or not being able to find another job, for the security of things staying the same. They feel safer just staying where they are. This "safety" can be an illusion. That scarcity-minded person is actually more at risk staying where they are. They are hoarding their talents, limiting their opportunities, and sacrificing their relationships, and they may ultimately become bitter and depressed, leading to health issues, problems at home, and a whole range of negativity rippling throughout their life.

If, instead, they were open to trying a new company or a new job or venturing out on their own, they would likely be better off in the long run. There is so much opportunity in the world, opportunity that may provide more income and even a greater, more fulfilling life. Sure, the transition might be a bit uncomfortable at first, but the reward could be enormous: a life lived in abundance instead of scarcity.

* * *

Everybody has scarcity in their life. Even people who seem to live in abundance can in truth be living in scarcity. This may sound counterintuitive, but the mindsets of scarcity and abundance actually have nothing to do with the amount of money you have. You can be the richest person in the world and still be limiting yourself by living in a scarcity mindset. A scarcity mindset keeps you in a cycle of fear. You fear that you're going to run out of money and not be able to live the life you want, so you focus all your work and energy on money—and never get to live the life you want.

I often meet people who are completely paralyzed by their scarcity mindset. They're so afraid of losing their money that they don't do anything with it. I see people who have enough money to retire and never even touch their savings, yet they are still afraid. They're afraid to lose what they have. They're afraid a competitor's going to come into their space and take away their business. They're afraid the government is going to change the rules and take all their money. The fear of losing their money causes them to stop doing what got them there in the first place.

People with a scarcity mindset don't have the ability to think abundantly about what they could do with their capital as they make it. They don't know what to do with their money, so they don't earn interest on it. The lost opportunity of compounding that money becomes significant. At JarredBunch, a lot of our work is showing people how to discover when they are in scarcity and create more results as they embrace abundance. With this newfound abundance we can address money from a new perspective where it can work for them instead of being locked away, doing nothing.

A scarcity mindset makes you fear that someone is going to take away your money, because the scarcity mindset says that the world is a zero-sum game, with only a finite amount of money or resources to go around. If you are winning, it means I'm losing. If you have something, it means I don't have it.

Abundance is the opposite of scarcity. Abundance says that all resources are plentiful. Abundance says that you can take advantage of any opportunity that presents itself. Abundance says that if you are adaptable and nimble, you can be whatever you want to be. Abundance says that if you dream it, if you believe it, then you can achieve it.

* * *

The first step to hacking your financial future is to hack your mindset, turning it from scarcity to abundance. You may be in abundance in one area and not another. This limited belief creates limited joy or results; it creates limits with your money too.

That's why, when we meet with a new client, we always start with mindset. The first thing most financial advisors do with a new client is take a risk-tolerance assessment. At the beginning, I could care less about risk tolerance. I'm trying to figure out where you are mentally. What's your self-awareness assessment? Where do you want to go? How do you see the world? What do you really want, if money were of no concern and if there were no obstacles to having the life you truly want? Once we figure that out, then we can determine what your risk profile really looks like and start constructing your financial plan.

Mind-over-Money Game

We are in the mind-over-money game. Money allows you to do things. It is the catalyst to enable you to achieve the things you want. If you don't have a clear understanding of what you really want, then it doesn't matter how much money you have. If you don't identify where you want to go, money by itself will never get you there. Without the right mindset, you'll never be able to radically hack your financial future.

Just as athletes can't win a game or competition until they get their mind right, you can't win the money game until you get your mind in line. LeBron James wasn't as successful until he played with Dwayne Wade. That's when the championships came. You can't win the financial game all by yourself or with a bunch of scrubs. What changed for LeBron? Who he was spending time with. That impacted his mindset and his results.

Think of the Kobe scowl or the Jordan confidence or the stoic calm of Larry Bird. You knew who was winning just by looking in their eyes. They knew they were going to win, and their mindset gave them the power to do so. The mindset matters over the game. It doesn't matter how skilled you are; if your mind is messed up, you're going to fold when it matters most. If you are confident in your success, you will have the power to succeed.

How can you have that type of confidence in your day-in, day-out life? Through a mindset of abundance. The difference between successful people and unsuccessful people is being able to identify when you are in scarcity mode and getting out of it immediately.

Take Mondays. Most heart attacks happen on the crossover from Sunday to Monday. When you live in a scarcity mindset, Monday morning means the stress is hitting. All the world is coming down on you, and the anxiety sets in. The scarcity person says, "I can't," because of this excuse or that excuse. The abundant person says, "I'm going to kick Monday's ass. This is the best day ever, and I'm so grateful to have the opportunity to crush it this week."

Retirement = Taken Out of Use

Retirement is another perfect example of a scarcity mindset. The definition of retired is taken out of use. I'm pretty sure that most people don't want to be taken out of use. I see people sell their businesses and retire with piles of cash, and within a month, they're ready to jump out a window (figuratively of course, because they get stir crazy). Never retire from purpose. Retire from scarcity, and delegate the things you hate so you can stay engaged. Why? Because if you retire without purpose, you won't know what to do with yourself. You'll get stuck. When people tell me that their goal is being able to retire, I say, "Great! Then what?" And people often don't know what to answer. They were thinking of retirement as the endpoint.

Abundant people are independently wealthy (as defined by them) and definitely not retired. They see themselves as still "in use." There's no one-size-fits-all answer to what to do after retirement. Some people want to travel and see the world. When they come back, the world looks different, and they want to help. Some people want to spend all their time with their families and/or teaching/enhancing the next generation. Some people pick up a new hobby or give back to the community. And some people find that what they actually want to do is what they've always been passionate about—their work.

Most entrepreneurs love what they do. And if they plan properly and surround themselves with the right people, they never have to retire from it. They can continue having fun doing what they love, because they have created a structure that allows them to go on building and enjoying what they've built. And they get paid to do it. Now that's the ticket! Abundance is knowing that retirement is not the end of the road. It's the start of a new road, with a world of new opportunities and options.

* * *

Flip It

So, how do you flip your mindset from one of scarcity to one of abundance? It starts by realizing that you are in the "want" business, not the "need" business. What do you want? What are all your possibilities for an ideal future? If you don't know where you want to go, then someone else is going to take you there, to a place not built on your terms. You are on a path right now, but is it your path? When you shift to an abundant mindset, you can tell the world, "This is exactly what I want." You start to create your unique journey, the path you want. The hack is on. What is it you can deliver to the world better than anyone else? A world of abundance allows you to identify what makes you great, be comfortable with it, and just be you.

Thinking abundantly means investing in yourself first—and then creating the systems and processes to take advantage of that investment. Part of that investment is in who and what you surround yourself with. I have found that most people are as good as the books they read and the people they hang out with.

It was only when my family moved out of subsidized housing and into the suburbs that I noticed people who were actually different, who weren't living in scarcity. Sports was my ticket to a different life. I had the opportunity to play football and had coaches who said, "Let us help you." That's all it took for me to start down the abundance track. I started hanging out with my teammates and found myself attracted to successful people and their families. Do you have someone who is coaching you when it comes to abundance, who knows you intimately before making a single financial recommendation? That is what Future Hack is about.

Just Do It

In college, I had the opportunity to travel the world. I maxed out my credit cards and student loans and took all the money I could muster from waiting tables and cleaning carpets. I wanted to experience the world. I spent a month in mainland China and Southeast Asia. I saw Egypt and the poverty up and down the Nile. I witnessed a government coup in Peru. I learned what a siesta was in Europe and saw thriving cities like Hong Kong, London, Singapore, and those of the United Arab Emirates.

When I returned from that trip, my eyes were open to all the possibilities that lay ahead of me. On the way home from the airport, my car broke down. I didn't even care. I literally tossed the keys to the guy working at the gas station. "You want a truck?" I said. A buddy picked me up, and I set forth on my new path. Game on! I was ready to go.

That's not to say everything changed overnight. It took work and some hard decisions. You can pick up a new mindset only if you let go of your old one. Even recently I had to be reminded of this lesson. Once, while we were in a business strategy meeting with my executive team on how to grow the business ten times, my business partner Lloyd Easters came up to me and handed me a cup. "Hold this cup," he said. Then he filled the cup with water. "Now," he said, "you can only use that hand, the hand that's holding the cup. Using that hand, I want you to pick up this pitcher of water." Of course, I couldn't pick up the pitcher of water because I had the cup of water in my hand. There was only one way I could pick up the pitcher: I had to drop the cup first.

> **You can pick up a new mindset only if you let go of your old one.**

In order to pick up something new, something bigger and better, I had to let go of old habits and ideas and even business relationships. The decisions were very painful. You spill a lot of water when you drop the cup. But they were the right decisions for the greater good of both our clients and our company as a whole. In order to pick up a mindset of abundance, you have to let go of the mindset of scarcity, of comfort and complacency. Because you can't have both. Being comfortable being uncomfortable is the sweet spot.

You Are Who You Hang Out with and the Books You Read

When I first discovered the abundance mindset, soon after I started my business, I tried to surround myself with abundant thinkers. At first, I couldn't understand why everything seemed so easy for them. So I started asking them questions. I started reading books on changing mindsets, like Rhonda Byrne's *The Secret*, which Kristina Rodriguez, my administrative assistant, gave me. As she handed it over, she said, "Man, you need some help," and she was right. Now I'm doing it, and she is too: she's no longer an administrative assistant, but a successful financial advisor helping others reach their full financial potential. I went to "therapy," in the form of programs like Dan Sullivan's Strategic Coach. He changed my life by providing me the structure to live an abundant life.

Coaching for your mindset is just like coaching in sports. When you're doing something wrong and a coach shows you the right position, you can feel the difference in your body. It's the same with mindset. There are many amazing thinkers out there who have spoken and written books on identifying and shifting your mindset, like Zig Ziglar, Ray Dalio, Tim Ferriss, Jim Rohm, Tony Robbins, and Gary Vaynerchuk. We have clients who have started healthcare networks from nothing and taken them public. Others who started out flipping homes with cash or credit cards and now own over a billion dollars in multifamily real estate. I've seen a small restaurant owner grow into a global, publicly traded restaurant chain conglomerate. His son is now following in his footsteps and doing it again. We have former NFL player clients who have created successful second careers in business. And a pharmaceutical rep who decided to leave and start developing surgery centers around the country. And more.

Abundance and success are all around us!

Once you start surrounding yourself with mentors—writers and speakers and people who think, "How can I do this?" instead of "I can't do this"—your thinking starts to change as well. When you see a problem, instead of thinking, "I can't do that," you start thinking, "There's a solution."

A scarcity mindset is always making excuses for why you can't get out of the situation you're in, why you can't move forward. An abundance mindset is knowing that in those excuses are the raw materials for the solution. The best companies in the world are created out of problems. For example, it was once a problem that there wasn't a nationwide market for goods, a place where vendors, brands, and businesses could all compete on one comprehensive free platform. The solution? An online platform, a little company you may have heard of: Amazon. Jeff Bezos saw the problem, took the raw material of that problem, and instead of making an excuse for the problem, made the problem into the solution. Now, as I write this book, Bezos is the richest person in the world.

Also as I write this, we are experiencing a global pandemic. The market is collapsing as local, state, and federal governments shut down businesses. This self-imposed recession will lead to innovation. There will be new services born out of this crisis.

"I can't" is not acceptable language at JarredBunch. We have a Dan Sullivan tool called Strategy Circle to formalize the discussion to get an optimum solution. "I can't" for us means "I don't know yet," which starts the debate for an answer.

Sadly, *can'ts* often come from the very people who are supposed to be helping you. Here's a secret: most financial advisors are more infected by scarcity than anyone. Many of them are trained by their employer—the financial institution—and typically the main focus of their training is on not losing Assets Under Management (AUM). The advisor is pigeonholed into playing on the financial institution's side versus playing on the client's side. The two agendas rarely align. With that mindset and structure, how are they supposed to help you achieve abundance? How are they supposed to help you apply an abundance mindset to your finances? It's the same with your typical CPA. I always joke that they are great employees of the IRS—very rarely do they actually look outside the box and think strategically while minimizing their clients' growth.

Don't Be That Guy

I've met with many high-net-worth clients who are surrounded by people with a scarcity mindset. And I end up spending most of my time shifting not the client's mentality, but that of their other advisors. I hear a lot of, "You can't do that because of this. It's not possible." And I spend a lot of time saying, "Why? Have you thought about this? What about this?" We try to not only coach our clients but also train the trusted advisor to think abundantly and comprehensively.

If you're in hypergrowth mode, if you want to do more and are seeking the life you really want to live, the people who are helping you need to share the same mindset. Even when someone is ready to change their life from one of scarcity to one of abundance, they often don't know how to implement that change and apply it to their lives. At JarredBunch, we love taking clients from the *needs* business to the *wants* business. *Needs* is the calling card to scarcity. It sets the stage for the minimum needed to survive instead of asking what is possible and what your ideal future really looks like.

Of course, the *wants* business isn't about freely spending all your money on whatever you want. An abundance mindset does not mean believing you have infinite cash. If you go out and spend all your money on Lamborghinis and mansions, you are going to lose the ability to take advantage of the future opportunities an abundant world would give you.

Lottery Ticket

Just take a look at the lucky people who win the lottery. They are given massive amounts of money, and in so many cases, it's gone almost immediately. Why? Because they didn't know what to do with it, how to manage it properly. They had the money, but they didn't have the mind—so none of it mattered. The same is often true with professional athletes. They get paid large sums of money, and yet a surprising number of them end up going bankrupt only three years after they retire. The ones who are successful, who don't go bankrupt, are the ones who are able to wrap their minds around their money, who are able to create rules, parameters, and barriers that allow them to grow.

An abundance mindset means knowing that you can take your money and make it work for you, so that you can continue both using your money and growing it. An abundance mindset means knowing that you can create more abundance for yourself. An abundance mindset says resources are unlimited, so you can always keep reaching and growing.

The Future Is Better than You Think

And the truth is, even if resources *are* limited, there is an unlimited number of ways to be resourceful and innovative and to use human ingenuity to find a more efficient way to Future Hack. This comes down to being able to shift the way we think. In their book *Abundance:*

The Future Is Better Than You Think, Peter H. Diamandis and Steven Kotler argue that with technological innovation, the whole world could be supplied with enough food, water, and shelter to give every person on the planet a high and healthy standard of living. All we have to do is rethink how we deliver food. In a controlled environment, you could feed the entire New York City area with only two skyscrapers. Crops could grow and be harvested many times per year. Just think what that would do for our environment—the scarce resource of food in many parts of the world could be solved with new technology. With an abundance mindset, opportunities to make the world better are endless.

* * *

Of course, it's easier to have an abundance mindset when things are going well. In the midst of a stressful life event—a sick family member, a divorce, a kid going into college—it can be hard to think about the bigger picture when you are focused on your immediate financial needs. The real trick is to have an abundance mindset when things seem to be going badly.

What Would Warren Do?

Warren Buffett's first business before he started Berkshire Hathaway did not work as planned: it nearly went bankrupt. Today he's one of the richest people in the world. Why? Because he didn't give up when things went wrong. He found new opportunities and turned his textile business into a conglomerate of investments in other businesses, including Coca-Cola and American Express. He didn't get stuck in a scarcity mindset. He said, "Let's go invest in some cigar butts. A cigar butt found on the street that has only one puff left in it may not offer much of a smoke, but the 'bargain purchase' will make that puff all profit." Buffett said that a company about to go down with some assets and tremendous value for growth in the future is like that cigar butt. That concept turned into the company that owns some of the most recognized brands in the world. His abundance mindset allowed him to see that there were more opportunities ahead of him.

Touch the Hot Stove and Love It

Some people invest in the market once, make a wrong decision, lose some money—and then give up. They feel the pain of being burned and decide never to invest in the market again. They typically lose due to a lack of methodology or the lack of due diligence or because they weren't shown how to Future Hack. To me, that's like going through a bad breakup and deciding, "I'm never going to love again. I'm not even going to try." That's a life of scarcity; believing that because you had one bad experience, it's not worth ever pursuing that thing again. I see this with people all the time—they lose, and then they don't ever go back and try again. Many people lost millions of dollars in the Great Recession of 2008 and 2009 and just gave up and let their emotions take control, missing out on the most unbelievable bull run in the free market economy. Many are going through it again now in 2020 with COVID-19 and its impact on the US and world economies. Event driven declines are very different from market driven recessions. What we don't know is if we'll push ourselves into a full-blown recession. Time will tell. What we control is how we respond. Plenty of innovation, new opportunities, and new services will be born out of this crisis.

A life of abundance says there's always another chance, that there are other fish in the sea. It says there are other opportunities in the market, as long as you're willing to take the time to understand. It says never give up. Living in abundance is knowing that even if you lost everything, you would still have *you*, your most important asset.

A life of abundance says there's always another chance.

Abundance means knowing that you can re-create yourself, find new opportunities, build yourself up again, and move forward.

The only constant in the world is change—and that's certainly true in the world of finance. If you live in a world of scarcity and something goes wrong, it seems like all is lost. In a world of abundance, if something doesn't go as planned, you are able to adapt, to pivot to an option B or C or D. Living in abundance means being nimble and adaptable. It means that even if something is not going your way at the moment, you are able to reposition your yourself and your finances to see and take advantage of the opportunities that arise from the situation.

Someone with a scarcity mindset looks at successful people and says, "That person just got lucky." An abundant thinker knows that luck is simply what happens when preparation meets opportunity. An abundant thinker knows opportunities are everywhere and makes sure they are prepared to seize them as they arise. Thinking abundantly is learning to see the opportunities all around you.

An abundance mindset allows you to dream, to set goals, and then to work toward those goals. An abundance mindset thinks about the *why*. What purpose can your money serve that is more important than the money itself? What do you want to *do* with your money? *Why* do you want money? Starting with why (to borrow a phrase from Simon Sinek)[1] will make your financial journey infinitely more successful. If all you focus on is the money, you're not going to get anywhere.

---

1   Simon Sinek, *Start With Why: How Great Leaders Inspire Everyone to Take Action* (New York: Penguin, 2009).

Living for Others

Living in a world of abundance enables you to follow your passion—your *why*. One of our clients, Victoria Frazier, loves dogs, so she started a dog rescue—"Love Is Fur Ever Dog Rescue." She found a pit bull that had been beaten nearly to death from a dogfighting ring. The poor dog, Abigail, was left to die on the street and was missing half her face and ear. Victoria had little money to help with all the surgeries Abigail needed. Since Abigail's head needed to be bandaged up, Victoria covered her head with bonnets. The word spread about Abigail, and "Bonnets for Abigail" was formed, starting a movement of awareness of and help for dogs like her around the world. Bonnets started pouring in, and Victoria's dog shelter was suddenly in the news. Revenue started flowing in: people were donating and coming in to adopt dogs. She ended up with an incredibly successful business, and Abigail was named the 2017 American Humane's hero dog of the year. And it all came out of her saying, "I just want to take care of dogs," and knowing she could follow that dream.

Every day I meet people with similar stories, people who believed that the world was an abundant enough place that they could create lives for themselves doing what they loved. Obviously, you have to do the work. These dreams don't come true by themselves. But as long as you're working, wouldn't you rather be working toward something you truly love and believe in?

It's easy to forget how good we have it. It's easy to only look at the negative things in our lives instead of counting the positives. The fact is, there is no better society in the world in which to live in abundance than America, in a society that allows and encourages microbusinesses and entrepreneurs to grow. Our system is set up to support those who seize opportunities and believe in a better future for themselves and their families. To live with abundance is to live with optimism. An abundance mindset is knowing that when you have a free market and a free economy like we do here, anything is possible.

CHAPTER TWO

ALWAYS EVOLVE

The cousin of abundant thinking is adaptability. What can you do better than what you're currently doing? What does your ideal future look like? What are your strengths? What are the opportunities before you?

Future Focused

Successful people live in the future, not the past. When you can think positively about the future, you can put yourself into a position to achieve that future. Many successful people create vision boards, a physical visual representation of their future. One of the best books I've ever read on vision boards is John Assaraf's *The Vision Board Book*. John built RE/MAX into a global real estate franchise right here in Indianapolis. Successful companies look to the future as well for ways to disrupt and transform their industries.

You can't change your future unless you can imagine what the future might look like. All the obstacles and things you don't like now are the exact things that need to be blown up. If you're not thinking about those things and making change, then you are living by other people's terms. Or, as I like to say, if you're not evolving, you are dying.

> **If you're not evolving, you are dying.**

* * *

Abundant thinking is the foundation for evolution. An abundant mindset allows you to see the opportunities you have to grow and change. We've talked about visualizing your future, about knowing where you want to go, what you want to do. But visualizing your future doesn't mean locking yourself into that future. You can keep developing those goals, those *whys*. They don't have to stay the same for the next forty years of your life. That's a scarcity mindset: the belief that you have to stick to the plan you've made no matter what, that you can't look for other opportunities because you've already committed to one set course of action.

If you ask a group of kids what they want to be when they grow up, they'll tell you they want to be astronauts, firefighters, football players—or Batman or Thor or whoever they saw at the movies last week. And some of them may grow up to be some of those things (OK, maybe not Thor). But as we grow up, most of us evolve out of those childhood future plans. So why would we think that we can't continue to evolve, that our plans at thirty might not be the same as our plans at fifty or sixty?

Our futures are much more dynamic than they used to be. The days of going to school, getting a degree, staying with the same company for thirty years, and then retiring with a pension are gone. Why would you sell yourself short by locking yourself into an unchanging financial plan in an ever-changing world? Why would you bypass all the opportunities that are going to present themselves to you, instead of evolving to take advantage of them? And as you get older, why wouldn't you want to evolve to incorporate the life experiences you have accumulated over the years? Why wouldn't you want to keep growing and finding new things that bring you joy and fulfillment? Why wouldn't you want to take advantage of your greater wisdom?

Don't Get Stuck

Many people get stuck not just where they are, but in the past. They get stuck reliving their high school glory days, they get stuck on something their parents did to them as a kid, or they get stuck believing that something in their past is holding them back. And so they stay stuck where they are, never changing, never growing, never evolving—stuck in the past.

The only person who can keep the past alive is you. It's your choice to keep living in the past or to move on to create a better future. If you can get out of that rut, if you can believe that the future is brighter than the past, then you can evolve. This is not to say you need to forget or ignore your past. In fact, the only true way to move forward is to accept your past and to be grateful for what you have achieved so far. Evolving doesn't mean erasing the past. Evolving means embracing and building on the foundation of everything you've done. Even if the road has been rough, you can embrace what you've learned from hardship and use it to your advantage.

Judgment-Free Zone

Some people who come into our office asking for financial help are embarrassed about their progress. We simply say, "Welcome to the judgment-free zone. This is your life's work up to this point; be proud of it! And now we can look to what's next. Let's build you a better future!" Today is only a snapshot. If you can't look back with gratitude, if you can't acknowledge your accomplishments, then it is hard to move forward. Acknowledging where you are now can make the present feel much more manageable, allowing you to move into the future. There's no better time to start than today. Because a year from today, you will wish you started today.

Some people get stuck in the past because they feel they've already peaked. Perhaps they were football stars in high school or college and feel like they'll never achieve those "glory days" again after a setback in another career or opportunity, so they stop evolving. In fact, they could take those past achievements and build on them. Those "glory days" can be a foundation for an even better future. Are you going to hit a ceiling and stop? Or are you going to break through that ceiling and reinvent yourself.

Part of evolving is saying, "I can change my future. I can change my situation." But if you want to change your situation, you have to be willing to transform yourself. I had to reinvent myself over and over again to get where I am today. I didn't like where I was, so I evolved—and sometimes, I had no choice but to evolve.

I was a football player in high school. All I wanted was to a play for a big-time college team. But then I blew my leg out in my senior year. I got a nice offer from a Division II school, but it definitely wasn't what I had envisioned for myself. However, I didn't sink into dwelling on the past, stuck on what might have been. I said, "Well, that path is closed. Since I'm not going to be in the NFL, I'd better reinvent myself right now."

And today, guess what? Some of our clients are NFL players! I may not *be* an NFL player, but I get to hang out with them and help them build lives after football. It's not the vision I expected when I was in high school, but because I didn't give up, because I evolved, I'm still in the game in a different, more meaningful way.

I find that people tend to reinvent themselves every seven years. I certainly feel like I've gone through those cycles. I did my seven years of sports, then I did seven years of college and postcollege education, and now I've got this career as an industry transformer—and when another seven years are up, we'll see what I evolve into next.

Now, you may be reading this and thinking, "I'm happy where I am in my career. I'm happy where I am in my life. Do I have to reinvent myself?" Evolving isn't always about completely reinventing yourself and doing something different than you're doing now. It's about constantly learning, investigating, and improving.

It's also about knowing that things could change at any time and being aware of obstacles that could keep you from adapting to those changes. It's making sure that you are generally self-aware and ready to take advantage of opportunities when they arise.

Luck is what happens when preparation meets opportunity. If you're not ready to take advantage of those opportunities when they appear, then you are going to miss out on them. I can't tell you when those opportunities will happen, but I can prepare you to take advantage of them by making sure your finances are in order. Do you know your downside, and are you always thinking

> **Luck is what happens when preparation meets opportunity.**

of a future that is bigger and better than where you currently are? If you're not ready to evolve, you're going to miss that opportunity.

Reinvention doesn't only happen during your working life. In fact, one of the most important times for reinvention is retirement. When you retire, it can be easy to sit around thinking about how successful you were in your work and feeling like you are now useless. Instead, think about how great you can now be at something else. Retirement means putting something out of service. Your life at that point shouldn't be "out of service" but starting a new type of service. Retirement savings and investing should be about funding the next level of service you want to do.

So many people see retirement as the end of the story: I work, I retire, the end. But the truth is, in retirement you are still evolving. You are still adapting. You are still moving forward. Retirement isn't when you start dying; retirement is when new and different opportunities for you to live appear.

Your Soul Purpose

For people who have worked their whole lives, whose identities are built around their work, retirement can spark a crisis of identity. When someone's whole life has been defined by their work, retirement can leave them asking, "Who am I now?" This can be especially difficult for people who have spent their working lives attached to a system, like a government agency. They struggle to reinvent themselves, because their lives have been dictated by that system and they've never had to be an abundant or revolutionary thinker. They have to break out of that identity entirely in order to reinvent themselves in retirement.

Many people reach retirement, sell their businesses—and then find themselves completely bored. My advice to those people?

Reinvent yourself. Look at what other entrepreneurs have done after selling their businesses. Discover a *soul* purpose for your money that is more important than the money itself.

For some people, that new purpose is philanthropy: giving back by helping other entrepreneurs build businesses. One client of mine sold his tech company and then created tech incubators to help build up new tech ideas. Instead of calling it quits and just sitting around on his boat doing nothing, he allowed his entrepreneurial passion to take a new form. Now he can take all his new friends out on his boat.

The people who can answer the questions, Who am I now? and What's my *soul* purpose? can reinvent themselves and find a new purpose and passion. These are the people who live long, healthy, happy lives after retirement. Many people say, "When I retire, here are all the things I want to do," and when they do retire, they never do those things. They just sit around—and those are the people who die sooner.

* * *

We encourage our children to strive, to master sports and academics, to be future focused, to better themselves. What would it look like if instead of staying where you are, you decided always to better yourself? What is it that you want to do, that you've always wanted to do, that you've never had the guts to do? Why haven't you done it? Why are you stuck where you are? Why can't you take that dream you've always had and act on it now?

People make all sorts of excuses for not evolving. "I don't have enough money to leave what I'm doing now and look for something I really love." "I went to school for this" "I've already invested so much time." "It's too late; I can't change paths now." In their minds, they create insurmountable obstacles.

In fact, some of the most successful people in the world achieved great things later in life. Julia Child didn't premier *The French Chef*, the television show that launched her to international fame, until she was fifty years old. Samuel L. Jackson, although he had been acting since college, struggled with addiction and only played small roles before being cast in *Pulp Fiction* when he was forty-six; now he's one of the top-grossing box-office stars of all time. Classic comedian Rodney Dangerfield's career didn't peak until he was in his fifties as well. Vera Wang resigned from Ralph Lauren to be an independent designer when she was forty; her clothing has now become a red-carpet staple, and in 2013 she received a Lifetime Achievement Award from the Council of Fashion Designers of America. Momofuku Ando invented instant noodles—including the worldwide brands Cup Noodles and Top Ramen—in 1958, when he was forty-eight years old.

All these people—and many more who achieved great things later in life—could have said, "It's too late for me. I'm past my prime. I can't do anything new with my life. It's too late to achieve the success I want." But they didn't let those excuses hold them back. When is the best time to plant a tree? Thirty years ago. When is the second-best time? Today.

Many of the things you believe are holding you back are in your mind, a function of a scarcity mindset. A scarcity mindset encourages you to think, "Woe is me. I was dealt this stack of cards, and there's nothing I can do about it." An abundant mindset thinks, "I was dealt this stack of cards—how can I play them to improve my situation?"

Think of the athletes who come back to win games against all odds. When those legendary quarterbacks—Joe Montana, Peyton Manning, Tom Brady, Drew Brees, Aaron Rodgers—are down in the fourth quarter, they don't say, "Well, this is the situation I'm in.

There's no way to get out of it." They look at the obstacle in their path and find the solution. No matter where they are at the moment, most of the time they figure out how to position themselves to win.

I see many people from the low-income area where I grew up still stuck in those bad circumstances. But I also see people who said, "You know what? This sucks. I'm going to go back to school. I'm going to get a degree. I'm going to become a dentist," or whatever career they decided to pursue. They did the work, and they got out. They chose to evolve. The people who chose not to evolve, who said, "I can't do that for this reason and that reason," are still stuck.

I don't just see this where I came from; I see it all the time where I am now. I hear it in people's voices, in the way they talk, when they say, "I can't do this; I can't do that." When I hear people say that, I say, "Let's identify the reasons why you say you 'can't.' Let's write each of them down, and then let's find a way you *can*." Evolving means always finding solutions and not taking no for an answer.

Start with WHY

Instead of taking no for an answer, evolving means always asking *why*. When you start asking why, then you start getting to the raw material from which you can build a solution. When we were working with the broker-dealer, I had a lot of ideas for financial strategies that would benefit our clients. But when I took those strategies to the institution, I was constantly met with negativity. "You can't trade across a thousand accounts with a single click." "You can't execute that strategy because you would have to recalculate the risk tolerance for everybody." "We know those investment options are available, but they're not available on our platform, so therefore we can't do that." "No, you can't help that person raise money for their business or find the capital for that real estate deal." I constantly got objections, excuses for why we couldn't implement the strategies our clients desperately needed. But I wasn't discouraged. To me, the fact that the institution was telling me no meant I was onto something great. I saw those rejections as the raw material for a solution. As you can imagine, the relationship with the institution was over, and it was time to build our own platform to serve our clients.

* * *

Evolution isn't a one-time deal. As soon as you're done evolving through one challenge or one change, another one is going to come along. I have found that the most successful people never stop learning, never stop exploring, never stop evolving. Don't let excuses hold you back. If you take action, the ability will come.

It can be easy to get complacent, to think, "Things are good enough, so why work to get better?" But if you get stuck in complacency, the world will pass you by. Successful people realize when they are getting complacent and guard against that tendency. When I was stuck in that big corporate job, I could have made excuses about why I couldn't get out. I had no money; how was I supposed to start my own business? I had a steady job, a steady income—wouldn't it make more sense just to stay put?

But I knew I had to evolve. I knew I had to grow and change. I wanted to be an industry transformer. I wanted to be able to help people in a way that no one else could: by giving them the power of knowing that they, too, can be disrupters and transformers—that they can do anything they want to do.

I knew I couldn't do that stuck where I was. So I took a leap of faith—or actually, several leaps of faith. Going from working with a broker-dealer in an investment firm to creating my own registered investment advisory firm was a leap of faith. Being able to offer financial advice by creating our own financial curriculum was a leap of faith. Going from leasing a building to buying a building was a leap of faith. Writing this book was a leap of faith.

If your current environment is preventing you from evolving, change it. What books do you read? Studies show that if you read just ten books on a given topic, you could be considered an expert. All you could ever want to learn is in a book. You can literally transform yourself by reading. Who are you hanging out with? You are the average of the five people you hang out with the most. If the people around you don't want to evolve with you, then it may be time to leave them behind. You see this in some marriages: one person evolves, and the other person doesn't evolve along with them. The results are not pretty, which is one reason why divorce is so high. And the same thing happens with business partners, with institutions—and with financial advisors.

At the broker-dealer, I felt like they were solely trying to protect their own best interest. In fact, we had to disclose this on the back of our business cards, informing clients that we acted as a representative for the institution, not for our clients. We wanted to make money work for people, not the institution. If your financial advisor is an advocate for an institution, not for you, it can kill your mojo and take away your purpose and drive.

The right financial team will evolve with you. When we work with a client, we want to be their partner. We want to help our clients grow. We want to be your financial coach, your personal CFO. We want to help you not only create strategies but also keep your emotional behaviors about money in check and find the rules that work for you. We want to help you evolve to the next level. We want to be part of your tribe, part of your Future Hack.

Our mission is to educate, counsel, and guide our clients to help them reach their full financial potential. It's a lifelong relationship that is always evolving and expanding. At JarredBunch, we want to help our clients see what their lives could be if they were to live in an ever-evolving world of abundance.

CHAPTER THREE

HATERS GONNA HATE— SO BEAT 'EM AT THEIR OWN GAME

I n order to hack the system, you have to understand the system. In order to play the game, you have to know the rules.

Financial institutions operate by four rules:

1. Get your money

2. Get your money systematically

3. Hold on to your money for as long as possible

4. Never give your money back

They create processes and products to achieve these goals, taking the money you invest in mutual funds or other products, such as 401(k)s or annuities, and using it to advance their business and create wealth, all the while restricting your access to your money for their benefit. They put your money to work, and while they may create some wealth for you, they are more focused on creating a profit for themselves and their shareholders. The rules and agendas of financial institutions might not align with what you want to do in your life— and their agenda is going to take priority. If you don't have an agenda for your money, someone else for sure has one.

You may read this and think, "Well, that's the system. The cards are stacked against me. There's nothing I can do about it." But that's a scarcity mindset. An abundant mindset says. "If that's the system, then hack the system and make it work for you."

You can take what financial institutions do and apply it to your own life. But if you're going to hack your future for the better, you have to know the rules of the game. If you jump into the middle of the game without knowing any of the rules, you'll fall flat on your face.

* * *

It's remarkably easy to get stuck in the financial system. One of the first things that happens to most people when they get out of college is receipt of their first credit-card offer. You sign up, and you get a free T-shirt! And before you know it, you've racked up debt that you can't pay off. It's your first chance to establish credit, but nobody has taught you how to do that properly.

That's what happened to me—and I found out the hard way when I tried to buy a car. They saw how terrible my credit was, and they immediately said they were going to charge me 9 percent for the loan. What's more, I had to put my first car on a credit card just to get the damn thing!

That experience taught me how financial institutions work. It was my first lesson: if you don't have good credit, they're going to rip you off. And if you don't pay off your loan, they take back the collateral from you by force. I had to learn that through experience, because they don't teach it in school. There I was—a business major with a degree in urban development economics, and my own personal credit was a train wreck.

Student loans and buying a car are just the beginning of the credit journey. When you buy a house, when you buy a commercial space for your business, when you buy rental properties, when you buy out another business … if you don't understand how the system works, you're going to get completely stuck.

And that's part of the reason why so many people do get stuck in the system, mired in debt—they simply don't know how it works. They've got PMI (Private Mortgage Insurance) on their houses; they're getting hit every which way because they don't have liquidity. It takes a long time to get out of those situations, and unfortunately, many Americans are still there. That's why the mantra of so many financial gurus is "Get out of debt, get out of debt, get out of debt."

Getting trapped by financial institutions isn't just something that happens to naive college grads. I see my private wealth clients go to the bank to get a line of credit or to invest in their business, and the financial institution says, "I won't give you credit unless you put all your money in our bank and use our financial products." Many use outdated strategies, proprietary funds, and other products, because while the loan or credit may help the business owner grow, it simultaneously takes away all the owner's control.

The truth is financial institutions are fair-weather friends. Banks love to lend money when you don't need it.

They'll be there for you when you don't really need them, but when you're in trouble—good luck. If you go to a bank and say, "I need to get a loan, because I'm in trouble and I need money," they won't give it to you. But if you know this rule, you can plan for it. We build our financial strategies knowing the rules of the financial institution.

The truth is financial institutions are fair-weather friends.

If you don't know the rules of the game you are playing, you are going to lose. If you learn the rules, then you can learn how to win the game. You can take any hand of cards you are dealt and still succeed. If you understand an institution's agenda, you can make sure they're not taking advantage of you. If you understand your own agenda, you can make sure that the institution isn't diverting you from your goals.

Now, financial institutions are not malicious. They're not out to get you. They are just trying to make a profit with little to no risk like everybody else, and getting your money is how they do that. Financial institutions need to make profits in order to deliver the services that we use—and we need those services. They are the backbone of our free market society. If we couldn't get access to capital by borrowing it, we could never buy houses or cars, and we could never build businesses. In a free market economy, banks and institutions allow you to take advantage of opportunities that arise. At JarredBunch, we use financial institutions every day to create wealth for our clients!

Because financial institutions are essential, we have no choice but to deal with them. For the most part our financial system is very solid, and for that I am grateful. However, we can choose *how* we deal with them. We can learn the game and create our own terms and conditions that work in our favor. We want to understand how to use the rules of the game to our best advantage.

Many people don't trust institutions. In 2008 and 2009, a very successful Major League Baseball coach I knew was running around putting the minimum amount of money into every bank possible, just in case any of them defaulted. That was his attempt to ensure that his money was protected by FDIC insurance. That distrust is the same reason so many people have invested in Bitcoin and other forms of cryptocurrency—things outside the traditional financial system. The money at the bank is not there anyway; they actually loaned it out to other people for a profit.

Many people who were burned in 2008 and 2009 have turned completely against financial institutions. They refuse to get back into the market. I have met people who refused to put their money to work—and they missed out on one of the longest bull market runs in history, a run that has lasted over ten years. What they lost in the downturn is miniscule compared to the compound growth they could have had since then. They will never be able to recapture close to what they could have had if they hadn't shut the door on that opportunity.

This mistrust of the system is going to affect them forever, because they didn't have the right advice on how to get out of the situation they were in. Of course, their mistrust is understandable, considering what they've experienced. We want them to learn the system and understand markets so they know how to navigate the system and make it work for them.

If something bad happens, instead of giving up and turning your back on the game, figure out what went wrong. Learn everything you can about what happened. Determine what the rules are. And then use those rules to get back in the game and win.

* * *

So, what are the methods and strategies institutions use to build their wealth?

To start, institutions use scarcity thinking to lock down your finances so your money is stuck. Take a 401(k), for example. The money you put into a 401(k) comes out of your paycheck. You can't take that money back out of the 401(k) without being penalized until you are age 59½. Then, when you are allowed to take it out, you pay substantial taxes on it—so you'd probably be better off just leaving the money in there. Certainly, 401(k)s and IRAs are the most popular savings plans in the world.

Velocity of Money

Meanwhile, the strategies the institutions themselves are using to create wealth are often the complete opposite of the strategies they offer to clients. The strategies used by financial institutions are anything but static. In fact, financial institutions rely on *velocity* of money: taking one dollar and getting that one dollar to do multiple things. This is the opposite of what they're allowing you to do with your money.

How does velocity of money work? Say you deposit one dollar into a bank. The bank will take that dollar, go to the Federal Reserve, and borrow a multiple of that deposit—let's say six times the deposit. They take that six dollars and lend it out to multiple people: to a person buying a house, to someone for a credit card, to someone buying a car. Now, each of those people is paying the bank back on one of those dollars. The bank has used your one dollar to create a spread, putting it to use multiple times over and making money each time. That's power with low risk.

This is what financial institutions do; so why can't you do the same thing? Why can't you use that same structure, with low risk across the board? Why not see how fast your money supply system can work?

What would that look like? Well, you could put your money into an investment account that has market-like returns with low volatility and start building it up. Then you could get a low-interest-rate line of credit against the investment account. Then you take the money from *the line of credit* and buy a piece of property that provides monthly cash flow way over your debt service. Then, when the piece of property appreciates or you improve it for a higher value, you could go to the bank and refinance the property *and get your money back*. Now you have a new asset with none of your money in it and your money never stopped accumulating while you picked up the new asset. Your dollar has now done two things. This is how the game is played. Be the gambler: when you win, take your money off the table and play with the house's money. This is how many real estate developers got their start, using one dollar in multiple ways, creating different assets that all grow.

Real estate is just one example. I've used my whole-life insurance to execute this strategy and have expanded it to investments as well. You can take money that was in savings or a bond, earning next to nothing, and move it into a whole-life insurance policy that pays like a bond, with tax-deferred growth and a guaranteed interest rate. Moreover, the policy comes with benefits: if you die, the company pays out the full amount. If you become disabled, the company pays the premium. If you get sued, the money is protected from creditors. Structured properly, the investment would always increase. Every dollar that had formerly just been giving a return on a bond is now giving a return plus all those additional benefits.

Even though this is what institutions do, most individuals don't even consider that they could do the same thing with their own money. Most financial institutions keep a third of their tier-one capital in permanent life insurance policies. That's their tier-one capital reserve. And yet, people don't think of doing the same with their own capital, creating their own tier-one capital reserve. Most people just have their money sitting in a checking account, not providing any benefits or money supply.

Big companies also leverage their assets to buy bolt-on companies. They strip out the redundancies—you need only one HR department; you need only one CFO—and then create more revenue out of that company. When interest rates are low, you can go out and buy a company with a loan and create substantial revenue.

When individuals want to acquire a new asset, they often just cash out what they have in order to buy it. When they do that, sure, they'll have picked up this new asset—but they have lost all the future growth of that cash.

When I bought a building for JarredBunch, I had to have capital available. But I didn't want to stop the growth on my investment accounts from compounding. So, instead of liquidating my assets, I was able to use leverage against them in order to acquire another asset that would provide more income and control. Now I was able both to acquire this new asset and to maintain my compounding interest, without any additional out-of-pocket cost.

This type of leverage is how you create velocity of money while limiting risk. I've heard so many people say that debt is bad—while at the same time the financial institutions, real estate developers, car dealers, and affluent individuals are all getting rich off those same strategies.

There are all sorts of reasons given why we shouldn't use those strategies: the market is risky, interest rates could change, borrowing is toxic, etc. And it's true that if you don't have the tools, resources, and understanding of risk to know what you're doing, these strategies *can* be risky and toxic. You need a personal CFO who is going to walk you through these strategies so you can take advantage of the same opportunities the financial institutions do with your money.

INTEGRATION VERSUS SELLING

Why don't more firms encourage their clients to take advantage of these strategies? Most financial firms are pushing products rather than looking at the coordination and integration of financial products. They either don't want their clients to know that much, or it's simply too much effort. Possibly they think it's dangerous. We do know institutions want you to be dependent on them. They create a secret sauce and refuse to tell you the ingredients, because they don't want you to be able to make it on your own. They think if they give a client all the tools, that person will go away and do it on their own, and they'll lose their client.

I believe the opposite. I say we should give you every tool available to succeed, and help you learn how to use the tools. Even in our old sales system for financial planning, many of the tools were turned off for the client. Now, we've turned on all those tools. We give clients access to everything, so they can freely learn and stress test rules of their own plan as they develop their own thought process. We know that if we do a great job educating our clients, they will be able to make better decisions when confronted with financial issues and stress. If we teach them how to use these tools, we'll never lose them as a client. In fact, we know that once they see all the moving pieces and how complex the system is, they'll be even more inclined to have someone there to help them navigate.

When financial institutions get hold of your money, they

typically invest the money differently than they advise you to do. They're going to have cash-value life insurance policies for protection and liquidity. They're going to diversify their cash flow and balance sheets by buying businesses and real estate to increase EBITDA (Earnings Before Interest, Taxes, Depreciation, and Amortization). They focus on making money work for them by using OPM—Other People's Money—and OPT—Other People's Time.

We want our clients to have the money work for them and to have those same options. For example, momentum-based strategies are usually held for institutional hedge funds or accredited private investment groups. The technology was structured to put all the money into a pool and then manage the pool. In traditional financial firms, this is still the case. But we have technology that allows us to do separately held accounts, which enables similar strategies for individuals.

Do you need to run out and put your money in a life insurance policy or buy real estate? No, not necessarily. It's about understanding that the smart money and financial institutions are using strategies you may not even be aware exist. It's about understanding how free-flowing money and cash-flow investing can work. If your money is tied up and illiquid, if you can't move it, you'll eventually get jammed up and miss out on opportunities. Fast money usually wins, but you have to have access to your money and look beyond the traditional strategies that are offered to individuals.

At financial institutions, the money works harder than the institution does. That's why they can afford to have a bank on every corner. And that's the point we want you to get to: where your money is working harder than you are.

Of course, most financial institutions may not help you get there because they have their own agenda—getting and keeping your money. Most financial advisors work for financial institutions, so they are following the rules and agendas set by those institutions. They've been trained on what strategies to offer their clients, and that's what they deliver. Therefore, their advice is usually, "Buy my product." Whether it's an annuity or a life insurance policy or a 401(k) or a mutual fund or a CD, they want you to buy the product that is going to give them control of your money. It's basic retail, and you are the consumer.

You Are a Financial Institution

You need to shift from being a passive consumer to actively playing their game. When you're dealing with a giant financial institution that seems to be holding all the power, how do you stand up for yourself and make things work in your favor? By thinking of yourself as a financial institution. Learn how the rules are set up. Learn how financial institutions do things. Start to run your financial life the way institutions do. Create your own cash-flow banking systems, your own money supply, your own balance sheets and savings and investment plan. Create your own velocity-of-money techniques so you can use one dollar more than one way. Create all these things for yourself, instead of being at the mercy of others.

High-net-worth families usually evolve into their own financial institutions—and you can too! The people at the highest link of the financial food chain end up becoming the bank. They're lending for business, they're in private equity, they own real estate, they have other people paying them. and they have a rules-based investment strategy. They're flipping the system around and putting their money to work for themselves.

The affluent make themselves richer by playing this game; why can't you play by the same rules? We're taught that the affluent have access to investment strategies that we don't. Well, guess what: you *do* have access to those exact same investment strategies. And you shouldn't be afraid to use them.

Haters are gonna hate. Unsuccessful people don't like successful people. They try to cut them down. They say, "You can't do that. You can't be that." This comes out of the same scarcity mindset that says the world is a zero-sum game, that says if you're winning, I must be losing.

An abundance mindset looks at successful people and says, "I want to learn from them." An abundance mindset looks at financial institutions and doesn't say, "Let's burn them to the ground," but rather, "What can I learn from them, so that I can do it too?" Why not play by those same rules? Why not, instead of hating them, figure out which rules are going to get you where you want to go?

When I was growing up in subsidized housing, the general mentality was that rich people are bad, that they were just out for themselves, that they didn't deserve what they had. The truth is rich people have generally put in a lot of work to get rich. They've done things differently. They've been prudent with their money. They've studied hard and learned how to play the game.

Instead of hating those who are more successful than you, try to have an open mind. Try to understand why they did what they did, and how they got where they are. Don't shut your door to what you could learn from them, no matter how you feel about them as people.

In sports, there is an important mantra: "Be coachable." That mantra can also be applied to your financial life. Always be coachable. Always learn. Always be adaptable. I learn from my clients, from my colleagues, and from other advisors. Successful people are always trying to learn from everyone around them—especially people who are as successful or more successful than they are. Successful people are always learning so that they can adapt to the ever-changing world around them.

CHAPTER FOUR

ADAPT TO CHANGE

R ecently, my wife Laura read a book about survival. The book recounted different scenarios and how people survived—or didn't. In every scenario where many people died—burning buildings, sinking boats—there was one common theme: people doing nothing. The boat would be going down, water pouring in, and people wouldn't do anything. They wouldn't jump off the boat or seek other avenues to escape. They would freeze out of anxiety—and lose their lives.

The moral of the book is that you have to do something. Get out of the boat. Get out of the burning building. Don't stay put. The mentality of a survivor says, "Move! Take action; do something." A survivor adapts to the environment of the moment, rather than staying still and letting things fall apart around them.

Even if you're not in a situation as dire as escaping a burning building, adaptability is essential for survival. Very few things are certain in life, but one absolute constant in the world is change. And yet most financial plans don't factor in the inevitability and constancy of change. Most financial plans are built for a static, unchanging future that you set when you create the plan—in other words, a future you can't predict and which doesn't actually exist.

> A survivor adapts to the environment of the moment, rather than staying still and letting things fall apart around them.

You can project the future all you want, but you have to realize you have no real idea what the future will hold. In fact, I've found that as soon as a financial plan is in motion, life starts to change. Literally the next day, different variables start shifting dramatically. Many of these variables are outside your control. There's inflation and market volatility. There are unexpected life events—illness that affects your income, car accidents that affect your insurance rates, something breaking down in the house that you have to put money toward repairing.

Life isn't always going to go as you plan. It's going to have a lot of bumps and curves. It's never easy. There's no free lunch. That's why you have to constantly adapt—because the moment you sit back, you're going to be in trouble. Everything is moving so quickly you really have no choice. Plus, it's more enjoyable to keep moving than to just sit still!

One of the top reasons people fail in retirement is that they can't keep up with the changes that are happening today—never mind planning for the changes that will happen in the future. You need a comprehensive strategy, and it needs to be adaptable to change. Unfortunately, there are not many options out there for comprehensive, adaptable strategies. Fortunately, this is something we are addressing in this book.

Life Isn't Linear or Static— Why Should Your Plan Be?

Most traditional financial plans are built to be linear. There's a mathematical formula illustrating that if you have this certain dollar amount and this amount of return, you would accumulate over so many years and would have this estimated amount of money in the future. When you retire, you can take the "safe withdrawal rate" and all is good. There are a lot of financial products out there based on this linear plan. For example, you can put money into an annuity or a 401(k) or something similar, and a traditional plan will show a linear growth chart of what your account(s) will be worth in the future.

The problem with these products (traditional financial plans) is that they are static and only work on paper. The return selected for the plan is artificial. And it assumes the future is consistently positive. Neither assumption is correct. Therefore the plan is not correct. Also, when money is set aside to reach a certain goal, it's completely tied up. It's only giving you one benefit and return. It's not adjusting to the constant changes happening in the financial environment around it or the dynamic changes in your life.

Target Date Funds are a perfect example of this. The assumption is that as you get older, your portfolio is going to become dramatically less risk averse, because you will be pulling on it and you need that money available. The problem is, these funds are based on a longevity estimate of eighty-five years old, and today, there's a pretty good chance you're going to live longer than that. Your money may run out because it may be too conservative an investment.

Today, 94 percent of people live to age eighty; 66 percent live to ninety, and at age 100, a full 17 percent are still around. That means most people are living basically an entire working career's worth of time after they retire. It's going to be hard to get through that much time with just the money you've built up over your working life—and a static, risk-averse portfolio may not help you if you went on a different path and didn't fit in the box. Plus, how does it make sense to build a fund around a static number—the age at which you'll die—when you have no real idea what that number might be? This is a very difficult task, but the industry needed to find a turnkey solution that most people could just pick.

In modern portfolio theory, investment portfolios are typically designed to be static, buy and hold. In order to be risk averse, present day investment philosophies will have you buy 60 percent stocks, 40 percent bonds and hold that over a thirty-year period, in order to give you less risk in the market. Every quarter or so, you'll rebalance it, sell off the good stuff, and buy the stuff that's not doing so well with the idea that those will go up in the future. By doing that, there's less risk.

However, if your whole investment strategy is static, and the world is constantly moving, you are probably not putting yourself in the best position to alleviate drawdowns and risk while also capturing as much upside as possible.

Unfortunately, many people end up losing control of money in inflexible plans and products because that's what's available to them (or sold to them), and it's easy. For instance, the Department of Labor has set mandates on many retirement plans, dictating that this is the standard. They are trying to create a system that is seemingly good for the whole versus each unique, individual person. Corporations rarely offer pensions for their workers, so the burden now falls on the employee. The technology and fiduciary oversight are rarely available to support adaptable and alternative investment strategies. So you have to check the box and take whatever plan is offered.

Many people get trapped into these inflexible, static plans because the government has made them an automatic option when you start your job. There's a reason for this. If you're not going to bother getting a retirement plan together for yourself, at least you've got something. But if you don't want the retirement plan, you have to opt out. If you want to hack your future, you need to understand your current position and where you are before opting in. Once you contribute, the money is illiquid, you have penalties, and your silent partner Uncle Sam has his tax that is due.

It's not just the government that creates strategies to tie up your money. Financial institutions also create packaged solutions to control your money, yet they invest money the opposite way. In an ideal world we would have control of our money and have an investment strategy that adapts to our current situation.

We say your life isn't static, so why should you build a financial plan that remains fixed? As your life moves and adapts, your finances need to be nimble and adaptable as well. Put yourself in a position to adapt to constant change—not only during your working years but throughout your entire life.

The need to be nimble and adaptable doesn't disappear when you stop working. Things don't stop moving and changing. In fact, it actually becomes even more important to manage your money effectively when you retire, because now you actually have to use it! You can't just go static—because even if you stop moving, the rest of the world isn't going to. Your financial strategy should work even when you die. The rules should live on for multiple generations.

Follow the Trends

Most people are very bad with money. I say if it finds the checking account, it finds a home. It's spent. If your money is set aside where you can't touch it, locked up and out of your control, that could be a good thing. You don't have access to it, so you know it will be there later. However, it can also be a really bad thing, because it is not available for you to use to take advantage of opportunities that arise. After all, the world is changing more and more quickly. Do you really want to let your money just sit around, doing very little or nothing? As Warren Buffett said, "If money doesn't work while you sleep, you will work for the rest of your life."

Your investment strategy should not be static; it should be constantly adapting, constantly taking advantage of changes in the financial environment. Only by paying attention to what is happening in the moment can you take advantage of the opportunities that change presents. The best way to secure your future is to adapt to what's happening right now.

People want to invest in something that gives the best possible return with the least amount of risk. Investors also want control and the ability to take action—but what action and when? We studied scores of theories, strategies, and methodologies with our clients' primary goals in mind.

Eugene Fama, a Nobel Prize winner, and Kenneth French codesigned their Three Factor Model, an asset-pricing model that describes stock returns through three factors: market risk (or beta), size risk, and value risk. Of those three factors, we tend to tilt toward size (small outperforms large) and value, because that gives a much better likelihood of beating market returns, which you can use to grow your portfolio. Fama and French later added fourth and fifth factors: the profitability of a company and the quality of a company. Finally, there is a sixth factor, which few can execute: momentum, which we'll be talking about in chapter 10.

When you combine beta, size, value, and momentum, you have a very slim chance of underperformance. In one year, it's about 23 percent; in five years, about 5 percent; by ten years, it's down to 1 percent; and in twenty years it's down to zero.

1927 - 2017

	1-Year	3-Year	5-Year	10-Year	20-Year
Beta	34	24	18	9	3
Size	41	34	30	23	15
Value	37	28	22	14	6
Momentum	28	16	10	3	0
All Four (25% to each)	23	10	5	1	0

Underperformance defined as having a negative return over the time period measured.
Source: Buckingham Strategic Wealth

Why? Because each of these factors contributes to performance. The combination of all four gives you the greatest likelihood of positive performance over time.

Trend following, also known as momentum, is a strategy intended to capture the market upside when things are doing well, while also protecting against the downside risk when things aren't going as well. In fact, when we build an investment strategy, the first thing we want to do is reduce the downside risk. This is something most investors understand: you should start with the risk—what you can lose—before addressing what you can gain. That's the first rule.

When the market starts dropping, we were always taught to say, "Don't worry; it will come back up in time. We don't know when, but it always comes back." That's scary if our clients need the money now or can't handle the volatility. Instead, we can say, "Yes, here's the trend, here is what's happening, here are the adjustments we are going to make, and here is why." This approach will help manage the financial emotions and help keep people moving in the right direction toward their dreams.

Our trend-following strategies are evidence-based, using a well-defined set of rules with the goal of reducing drawdowns while capturing upside growth. If your portfolio experiences large drawdowns, you could lose years of upside, because it takes so long to recapture what you lost. Let's not forget the most recent lost decade of the early 2000s where the market had a return of zero for a period of ten years or more. In the worst cases, you might never come back if you had to draw on your portfolio during that time.

Why does it take so long to recapture losses? Because of the volatility gremlins. What the heck are volatility gremlins? They're what makes your money seep away without you even noticing.

Say you have a portfolio with $100,000. The market goes down, and you lose 50 percent of that money. Now your portfolio has $50,000. The next day, you gain 50 percent—so you're back where you started, right? Wrong! Fifty percent of $50,000 is $25,000, so now your portfolio has only $75,000, *not* the $100,000 you started with. If you lost 50 percent and gained 50 percent, technically your rate of return is zero. But the volatility gremlin has run off with 25 percent of your money. It's gone. The lost opportunity cost of not making an adjustment to counter that volatility is catastrophic. Some portfolios can take a decade or more to recover. If you have decades to recover, then it's not so bad; you just have to stomach the drops. But if you need the money, you face a significant risk, called sequence-of-return risk. You don't know when the drop will happen. And if it happens when you need the money, you are potentially in a world of hurt. When you draw down a portfolio that is dropping, it's called disinvesting, and it further decreases your likelihood of recovery.

If you understand velocity, you can avoid those gremlins stealing your money—and in fact, you can actually harness them to make money. There are always going to be downturns in the market. Historically, the markets are actually in drawdown a lot more frequently than you probably realize. From 1927 to 2020, the markets were in a drawdown about 50 percent of the time. Generally, people are not aware of this historical precedent. They are either ignorant of how the market works, or they just don't look at it. In fact, many major investment advisors will say, "Don't look at that stuff. It'll just drive you nuts."

We say, be cognizant of the trends and evidence behind what you're investing in. If you understand it, then you can try to capture as much of it as possible. Don't be afraid of downturns; understand them and harness them. Most super wealthy people created their money in bad times, not good times. The Rockefellers created their wealth during the Depression, because they created systems that worked. Economics is a cycle. Things get bad, then they get good again, then bad, then good. If you're smart, you'll take advantage of those cycles.

We did a back test recently to demonstrate how much money velocity can make you. If you put one dollar in the S&P 500 on January 1, 1998, by November 30, 2019, you would have earned 380 percent growth of your money. However, along the way, you would have had max drawdowns of around 55 percent, from which it would have taken about 1250 days or nearly 3.5 years to recover.

Now, let's say during that same period, you used a trend-following formula such as twelve-month moving average, two hundred-day moving average, or something similar. When the S&P

500 dropped below the moving average, you moved your money out to avoid the drawdown. By avoiding that large drawdown (approximately 20 percent versus 55 percent), your dollar would have grown 723 percent, instead of 380 percent. You would have double the amount of wealth because you didn't participate in those large drawdowns and your recovery period was shorter. You also didn't follow the worse course of allowing emotion to take over and selling at the worst time or never getting back in. And that's just on one asset or holding, since you can now purchase an S&P 500 ETF that holds all five hundred companies.

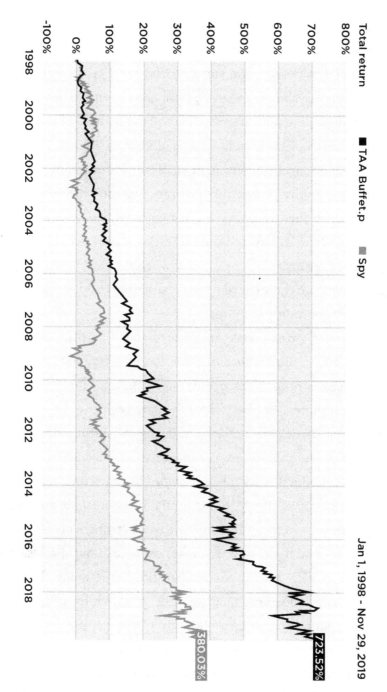

■ TAA Buffet.p   ■ Spy

Total return

Jan 1, 1998 - Nov 29, 2019

723.52%

380.03%

Source: Kwanti. Results are from back test and do not reflect any actual account.
Past performance is no indication of future performance.

Don't get me wrong, buy-and-hold investing does work. But the caveat for it to work is you must stay invested at all times. You must ride out all drawdowns. And you must stay invested for an extended period of time to allow for recovery from drawdowns. In our opinion, these are big asks of most people. That's also why the Dalbar Study—annual research of investment returns of individual investors—consistently shows investors getting dramatically lower returns than the market. A majority of investors just can't stomach the volatile ride of the market; therefore, they make emotional decisions with their money. In addition, buy-and-hold investing leaves you exposed to a sequence-of-return risk (for example, when the drawdown happens right before or right after you need the money) and longevity risk (outliving your money).

Of course, many people out there wouldn't put their money in the S&P 500 at all, because they are too afraid of something like that 55 percent drop. Some people are so afraid of the market they never invest in the first place. There's a whole segment of people who will just not participate at all. Instead, they're putting their money into CDs or annuities to protect against these drawdowns. And it's true, those products work when it comes to protecting you against drawdowns; but what are those insurance companies and banks doing with your money? The opposite of what you're doing: they're investing or lending it. And that takes us back to our discussion in chapter 3: if it's what the financial institution is doing, if they're making money off your money, why can't you do it for yourself?

If you know how to take advantage of change, if you can adapt to it, you can greatly increase your wealth. If you don't adapt to changing trends, or if you are so scared of change you stay out of the game all together, you are going to miss out on big opportunities.

Embrace Change

Of course, constant change is unsettling. It can often lead to stress, to losing confidence in your financial strategies, to feeling uncertain about the direction you're going. This anxiety about whether you're doing the right thing, this discomfort, can lead to disorganization. You start to believe that you're not in control. You start making illogical decisions based on emotion—both bad emotions and good ones.

It's a psychological cycle. People don't know how to be content with where they are, so they end up in a vicious cycle of optimism, excitement, thrill, and euphoria crashing into anxiety, denial, fear, desperation, and panic.

How do you avoid this stress, anxiety, and disorganization? By embracing change. Accept that change is constant. Don't be afraid of it. Be okay with it. Be ready for it. If you can embrace change, then you can be content with where you are, because you know you are in a position to adapt to whatever comes next. Focus on being optimally balanced where you are and positioned to adapt, knowing that the future is going to look radically different than the present.

> **Accept that change is constant. Don't be afraid of it.**

When people think of change, they usually think, "I have to figure out how to withstand it." But that's actually not the right mindset at all. Instead of thinking about withstanding change, think about how to embrace it and take advantage of it. The same goes for your financial plan. It's not just about having a plan that is able to adjust to change; it's having a plan that is *meant* for change. It's having a plan that actually takes advantage of change. You know that change is going to happen; build your plan around that inevitability.

How? By always positioning yourself to adapt. When you're playing basketball, you're best served if you catch the ball in a triple-threat position—a position from which you can do three different things: shoot, drive, or pass. Then, when you get the ball, you're in a position to make a judgment call based on the situation in front of you and make whatever move is best at that moment. You don't know what that move will be until you get the ball—but when you get the ball, you are ready to go, no matter what the best move is.

The same is true in financial planning. Planning needs to be about positioning yourself for the current day *and* making sure you're positioned properly to adapt to the inevitable changes that will come. You can position yourself so that when change hits you, you are able to make whatever move is best to adapt to that change.

Of course, financial planning isn't exactly like basketball. After all, in basketball there's a countdown clock. You know exactly how much time you have left to win the game. In life, there is no countdown clock. You have no idea how much time you have left, when the game is going to end. Should you go really hard right from the start, because the game could end quickly? Or should you pace yourself because the game might go on for a long time? How are you going to play the game if you have no clock?

We can't control the countdown. We can't control how much time we have left. The only thing to do is to set what we can control: the rules we play by, that we can stick to as we go. In order to create a financial strategy that is both stable in the present and malleable for the future, you have to ascertain a set of principles and rules to live by—something we'll discuss in greater detail in chapters 8 and 9. If you have a comprehensive rules-based system for the way your money is managed and you abide by those rules, the stress that constant change would normally put on you diminishes and becomes easier to deal with.

If you don't have an investment strategy that you know you can stick to for the long haul, you're going to bail out when things get scary. If you have a rules-based investment philosophy, you can adhere to that agenda no matter how the markets are moving. If the market drops, you've got a rule that allows you to choose which move is best: sit and hold on, rebalance, exit and try the next best asset class ... Whatever move is best for that situation, you are ready to make it—without gambling away your money or putting yourself in a worse position!

Once you make the move, once you either pass, shoot, or drive, you don't go static. Once the ball is out of your hands, you figure out which move is best to reposition yourself so that you're ready for the next time the ball comes to you. We do the same thing with money. After you've made that move, what are the new opportunities that might not have been there before?

Keep Your Money in Motion

Opportunities are created by money in motion, not by money sitting static and inflexible. Money is like blood. If it's moving, you're all good. If it clots and stops moving, you've got a big problem. As we talked about last chapter, most wealthy individuals and institutions make their money using the concept of the velocity of money: how many times you can use one dollar, how it can move, how it can do many different things.

Opportunities are created by money in motion, not by money sitting static and inflexible.

If you don't put your money to work, it will erode. You want to keep your money in motion, so that you can keep your ability to be nimble throughout your life. Keeping your money in motion allows you to seize new opportunities as they arise and avoid certain dangers. It helps you understand what strengths you have and how you can take advantage of them as well as what weaknesses you have and how you can protect against them.

You want to keep your money moving, rather than putting it in a plan, setting it and forgetting it, and then trying to open it up thirty years from now. Instead of setting and forgetting, you should be monitoring your financial data. Understand the ebb and flow of what's happening. Use investment strategies that adapt to the trends of the marketplace. Have a long-term focus, but know what is happening in the short term too.

Having an adaptable financial plan is what allows you to adapt not only to changes in the financial world but also to the changes that might happen in your life. Whether it's good changes, like having kids, or unfortunate changes, like accidents or illness, things are going to change, and you have to be able to adapt.

When it comes to unexpected life changes like accidents or illness, even if you have all the proper insurance coverage, you still need to make sure you have the money available to address the costs that arise. Your financial plan doesn't just need to be flexible to cover those short-term life events, like a car accident or an injury. It also needs to be able to adapt to long-term life changes. Perhaps you weren't planning on having kids, but then things change and you do. Can your financial plan adapt? Perhaps you have an accident that causes a lifelong disability. Or perhaps you have a child who has a disability. Can your plan adjust to accommodate your or your child's care—potentially a lifelong expense?

Unfortunately, many people's plans are so inflexible that, when they are faced with situations like these, their finances fall into chaos. But if you have built your plan on evidence-based rules and principals, you can adjust your plan to continue to operate by those rules and principals, while adapting to these long-term financial considerations.

The first thing we do to create the flexibility needed for those life events is to create different buckets of money from which to pull in the event of an unexpected life change. Bucket 1: Have a three- to six-month reserve fund. Bucket 2: Have an account designed for minimum volatility for about a year of liquidity. These reserve funds give you liquidity that you can access immediately if one of these unexpected situations arises. That way, you may never have to tap into your retirement accounts, or get a line of credit on your house, just to get through whatever issue or challenge you're facing.

Once you have a year's worth of liquidity, Bucket 3 is money put into investment accounts. These accounts are long-term focused and could be both taxable and tax-deferred. Applying evidence-based investment philosophies allows portfolios to be more adaptable to the ebb and flow of the market. Using a diversified combination of value, size, and momentum, you can build your financial plan out in such a way to minimize volatility that can rob your account and create a smoother investment ride to meet your goals.

Make Sure Your Vitals Are Healthy

Financial strength doesn't just come from a good investment strategy. You have to make sure your financial vitals are strong and healthy. I see people all the time who haven't set up their finances properly. They didn't build up their six-month reserve. They don't have a year of liquidity. They don't have a proper business plan. They haven't been saving. They aren't protected. They don't have their financial statements set up in such a way where they can get leverage to be able to take advantage of a business opportunity when it comes along. They're just not prepared, and they will fail.

You have to get the foundations set up before you can really play the game—and that's exactly what we'll be talking about in the next couple of chapters.

CHAPTER FIVE

CONTROL YOUR CONTROLLABLES— PROTECT YOURSELF!

We know the world is full of constant change. Many things are out of our control. No matter what we do, we are going to be at the mercy of certain unexpected events and sudden shifts. But that doesn't mean you have to resign yourself to whatever happens. There are certain things that are controllable—and if you can control your controllables, you can win the game.

You could walk out the door tomorrow and get hit by a truck. You have no control over that. But you can control what happens if you do get hit by a truck and protect yourself, your income, and your family. You can't control an unavoidable car accident and/or if someone decides to sue you, but you can control the amount of liability coverage you have. You can't control becoming sick or disabled, but you can control your health and disability insurance. You can't control death, but you can control what will happen to your business and assets when you pass away.

You can't control everything that happens to you in life, but you can control whether you are prepared for whatever comes. Protection is really the one thing you can control. Controlling your controllables is the foundation, the bedrock, of your financial plan. Protection is what gives you control, what lets you set the game board and puts you in a position to win the game.

By protecting yourself and controlling your controllables, when somebody or something comes to challenge you, you are challenged on your game board, on the playing field you've set up for yourself. As I heard Tony Dungy, the former head coach of the Indianapolis Colts and the Tampa Bay Buccaneers, say once, "We have a game plan, and we impose our game plan on our opponent, not the other way around." That's our philosophy too. You set the stage, you drive the plan, rather than letting the uncontrollables drive for you.

Don't Neglect Protection

Lack of protection is one of the biggest issues I see. Even the most sophisticated and wealthy people out there often don't have sufficient protection set up—and what they do have is often outdated, because often they have evolved and the plan has not.

Why do so many people neglect protection? Well, for starters, most people look at protection as a cost, so they don't want to address it. They don't want to deal with one more expense. But beyond that, people often aren't even aware of what they lack. They haven't thought through the "what-if" scenarios and how they would protect themselves. If something were to happen, they would be in big trouble.

Of course, nobody wants to sit around and think about all the bad things that could happen. Nobody wants to think about illness, accidents, death. Nobody wants to think about what happens to their money when they die. Nobody wants to think about who would take over their business if they die. It's not a fun conversation to have. And when you have an expense that's not very pleasant to think or talk about, it often gets neglected.

Well, I have some good news for you: in order to protect yourself, you don't have to sit down and imagine every single terrible scenario that could possibly happen to you. Instead, you can protect yourself in certain critical areas. Make sure your liabilities are covered. Make sure your income can be replaced if something happens to you that prevents you from working. Make sure your family is protected if you die prematurely. Make sure your assets are under your control, not someone else's. Make sure all of these are covered for their full value—including yourself.

At the end of the day, if you don't protect yourself, you could end up stuck in a really bad situation. All of this will put you in a position to react to anything that could happen to you—whether it's something you thought of or something you've never in your wildest nightmares imagined.

Prepare for What Happens When You're Gone

Nobody likes to think about death, but unfortunately death is inevitable. Have you thought about what will happen to your wealth and assets when you die? I had a client recently whose father died suddenly in a horrible motorcycle accident. The father had no beneficiary designation on his retirement account, so his daughter ended up having to pay full tax on the withdrawals from the 401(k). All the wealth that the father had been working so hard for throughout his life got cut in half instead of all going to his kids. No one could have controlled the tragic accident; but if they had been prepared and protected, at least his money could have gone where he wanted it to go after he died.

That's why one of the critical elements of protection is estate planning. Estate planning is not just for the uberwealthy; *you* need an estate plan to some degree. Estate planning is basically setting up ownership of everything so that all your assets go exactly where you want them to go when you die. Structures like LLCs (limited liability corporations), trusts, and wills are designed to protect you and your assets. You can do the same thing for your business, setting rules and a plan for what should be done if something happens to you.

> **Estate planning is not just for the uberwealthy; you need an estate plan to some degree.**

One common estate-planning strategy today is using dynasty trusts as a way to put money away for multiple generations if something happens to you. These trusts can protect you from creditors and estate taxes, and you can set rules to make sure your money goes to whom you want, under your terms and conditions. These structures give you the ability to be nimble and adaptable to most wealth-eroding circumstances.

One thing that can—and hopefully will!—happen is continued growth. I find that successful people continue to be successful, so your worth and assets are always growing into something much bigger than they are now. As you grow and evolve, your wealth increases. Prepare for that future by protecting yourself today, knowing that things are going to change. If you own your assets in a creditor-protected and tax-friendly environment, it could allow your wealth to multiply and benefit many generations to come.

One form of protection that could adjust as you go is life insurance death benefits. If set up properly, benefits could increase throughout time and can keep up with inflation pressure in the future. You can put future increase options on your disability policy that allow your income replacement to ratchet up as your income grows. These types of built-in adjustments protect your future self as you continue to grow and be successful, even if your health and insurability change.

This kind of protection doesn't just save you money; it can also create more wealth for you. In fact, if you insure your value, you can actually spend more of your money and use the insurance to replace it in the future—something we'll be discussing in more detail in chapter 7.

Protect Your Assets

The next major element of protection is protecting your assets. That includes protections like car insurance, homeowner's insurance, and general umbrella liability coverage that covers your car and your home, which can also protect against frivolous lawsuits.

This kind of coverage is certainly an expense, but it's a necessary one—and there are ways to defray it. If you have enough money saved up (and we'll come back to saving in the next chapter), you may be able to self-insure the small risk and have the insurance company pick up the catastrophic risk. You may be able to increase your deductibles, which brings down your premiums, and use those savings to buy an umbrella policy for a million dollars, which typically costs two or three hundred dollars a year.

Insurance companies, like all the financial institutions we talked about in chapter 3, have their own agenda, which is to charge you as much as possible while giving you the least amount of coverage. If you have low deductibles, you probably also have low liability limits—meaning, if something catastrophic happens for which you need liability coverage, you'll likely be on the hook for a large portion. Your goal should be to have the most coverage for the least cost, which is the opposite of the insurance company's agenda. One of the best ways to do that is by self-insuring the small risk (i.e., high deductibles) and having the insurance company pick up the catastrophic risk (i.e., max liability coverage).

However you structure it, protecting your assets is essential. You can't necessarily protect yourself from an accident, but you can control what happens afterward and protect yourself, your income, and your family. As careful and cautious a driver as you might be, sometimes things can go wrong. The road could be icy. An animal could dart across the road. Something out of your control could happen that could cause you to hit someone, or someone could hit you. If you are liable, are you protected?

Your coverage doesn't just protect you if you are liable; it can protect you if the other person is liable as well. You can't rely on the other person to have insurance or liability coverage—or even if they do have coverage, that it will be enough to truly protect you.

Let's say you're a forty-five-year-old making $100,000 a year and you get hit by a Budweiser Beer truck and can't work anymore. To cover that lost income for the rest of your life, you'd need a minimum of $2 million ($100,000 per year for the next twenty years of your working life)—and that's only if you're assuming that you'd never make more than $100,000 a year for the rest of your life. A big company like Budweiser would have enough liability insurance and assets to cover that with no problem.

Now, imagine you got hit by someone who only had the state minimum of coverage, which is only $25,000 of liability coverage in most states, or worse, no insurance at all. In that case, you would want to make sure you have enough liability to cover your full human life value of a minimum of $2 million. If this were to happen, then you just self-insured yourself for $1,975,000.

This is why it's important to understand your human life value— so that you can protect your most important asset should the worst happen. If you get hit by that truck when you're in your twenties and can't work anymore, your human life value is the income you'd have made over the forty to fifty years of work you would have had ahead of you. If you get hit in your forties, that's twenty to thirty years' worth of income you've lost. How much are you willing to insure your value for?

Protect Your Income

This brings us to the next element of protection: protecting your income.

Your income is your most valuable asset, and yet many people don't bother to insure it for what it's worth. They insure their homes, their possessions, their cars ... in fact, some people spend more money on car insurance than on insurance to protect their income! They'll insure their car for $20,000, $30,000, or $50,000, and that same dollar amount could be protecting your most important asset, which is you! You want to protect your car, but shouldn't a larger priority be protecting your income, which generates the revenue you live on, that you used to buy that car?

If you've got a goose that lays golden eggs, what are you going to insure—the eggs or the goose that lays the eggs? While naturally you want to protect the eggs themselves, even more important is protecting the thing that produces the eggs, so that you can accumulate more eggs. Your income is what allows you to obtain all those other things you are protecting—your house, your car, your possessions—your golden eggs. You should make sure you are protecting the goose—your income—as well!

Part of protecting your income is protecting yourself in the event that you should become disabled and can't work. Many people are severely underinsured when it comes to disability. Just like all those other hard conversations, people don't want to think about become disabled or incapacitated. I've heard clients say, "If I become disabled, just kill me." And yet I know plenty of people who have become disabled and are living full, good lives—and they're able to do so because they had the proper protections in place. They made sure their income was protected. They had disability insurance. If they didn't have those protections, their lives would be a lot more difficult.

Disability can come from both short-term and long-term illnesses. It can come from accidents that leave you either temporarily or permanently unable to work. A typical disability claim lasts between five and seven years. Imagine if you couldn't work for five to seven years. Would you and your family be able to survive financially? Without disability insurance, most people would be financially devastated. They wouldn't be able to pay their mortgage; they could lose their house; they could lose their health insurance; they would completely deplete their savings. It can be absolutely catastrophic.

Sometimes, even when you think you're protected, there's a little caveat in there, a little loophole, and you can fall right through. I have a close college friend who was doing really well in life: he had a good job at the top of his career, making the best money he had in his life. Then, he had an accident in a pool and became paralyzed. Another college friend of mine got in a motocross accident and broke his neck. Both of these friends were at the absolute top of their games—and all of a sudden, they could no longer do the work they'd been doing.

It was a rude awakening. They now had to do everything differently, because what they'd been so good at doing wasn't going to work anymore. Thankfully, each of them had some protections in place—but not complete protection.

The first friend I mentioned had just signed a contract with an amazing new job and was ready to start when the accident happened. This new job had disability coverage—but there was a thirty-day waiting period before he was eligible for coverage. It was the most unbelievable, worst-timing scenario you could imagine. In a perfect world, he would have had his own disability coverage that he bought separately from the employer, and his income would have self-completed. But that wasn't the case. There was a gap in coverage, and he fell through it. The good news was we had other protections in his life policy and other things that allowed him to form a very successful foundation and was able to help other families who have had similar hardships.

You can't rely on someone else to protect you. You have to create protections for yourself. If you have a controllable—like protection—don't leave it in someone else's hands. Control your controllables.

Protect Your Wealth

Along with protecting your income, you want to protect the wealth you've accumulated. When you put your money into something and put that savings away, where does it actually go? How much of it is in insurance policies that are uncorrelated to the market? How much of it is in an investment philosophy guided by evidence-backed rules? Are you protected? Or do you have a plan against those volatility gremlins we talked about who will come and steal your money? You have to be very cognizant of how volatile those portfolios are, because that money can seep out and disappear.

Set up your investment portfolios to reduce volatility by managing the downside through an evidence-based system using rules that follow market trends and to have an investment philosophy that's going to be with you for the long haul. That's what protects against volatility gremlins and gives you the ability to stay in the game with less exposure to the overall market.

Considering the end dollar first before considering the risk is like considering your offense without considering your defense.

In order to do this, you have to think of the risk of loss first. You want the evidence before you go in. Then you can set up downside risk protection. Most wealthy people and successful entrepreneurs think of the risk first, before they think of the return on the investment. Instead of thinking, "I'm going to buy that stock because I can make this much money," they start with the loss in mind. Once they consider the loss, then they consider the probability of success.

Considering the end dollar first before considering the risk is like considering your offense without considering your defense. I see people all the time who are so focused on the offense—i.e., growing their wealth—that they forget about the defense. But it's defense that wins championships, not offense. Remember, investing is all about ROI—return of investment.

Build a Nimble Defense

When people think of protecting themselves, when they think of a good defense, they often think of building some big, impenetrable iron wall. The problem with big, impenetrable iron walls is they make you completely inflexible. A good defense isn't about sitting still. Think of Floyd Mayweather; the reason no one can beat him is not because he's a big wall of a man with a killer knockout but because of his speed, his agility, his nimbleness. He may not hit as hard as some of the other guys, but he's so fast you can't hit him, so eventually he's going to win. His main strategy is not getting hit.

You want your defense, your protection, to be equally nimble. If you build a castle and surround it with a moat, sure, you're protected from invaders. But if you just sit behind those walls, eventually you're going to starve to death—and then those invaders can march right in and take your castle anyway.

You can't just build a castle. You have to build a stable, sustainable kingdom—and the same is true of your finances. You need to maintain complete financial balance. If you're leaning too far in one direction or the other, something's going to give. You are only as strong as your weakest link.

Most clients I see tend to lean too far to one side or the other on offense and defense. I recently talked with a new potential client who hasn't put money back in the market since 2008. That client has missed out on a huge run-up and will never see it again. What would a million dollars have looked like if they'd put it back in the market? It would probably be about two and a half million, had they done it right. Instead, they're worrying about how they're going to scrape by in retirement. Their money has spent all these years not doing anything, not keeping up with inflation, and now it's worth less, when it could have been two and a half times more. And it's not just the wealth lost in the past ten years; it's the future wealth lost in the next twenty.

That's the person sitting in the castle starving to death. If they had had a strategy that was legitimate, with rules they could stick to, backed by evidence, they could have made better decisions and been much better off today.

As we talked about in the last chapter, we have to be adaptable. We have to be nimble. We have to move. Our money needs to be free to invest in order to grow. It's possible to set up your protection in such a way that it makes you completely rigid, and then you become vulnerable, because you are unable to be nimble and adaptable to change. If you put all your money into CDs to protect against market risk, you'll have no ability to protect against inflation.

You can't just let your resources sit idle. You want to put them to work for you. If money sits on the sidelines doing nothing, if you have no strategy for it, something's going to steal your money away, whether it's a volatility gremlin or an inflation gremlin or another eroding gremlin.

Prepare for Downward Pressure

Money always has downward pressure. First, there's inflationary pressure. If inflation is at 3 or 4 percent, you know that one dollar today is going to be worth 50 percent less in twenty years. Therefore, the minimum dollar amount you need to maintain your lifestyle is going to be a lot higher in the future when you will really need it. Compare the costs of things today with what they were twenty years ago. The buying power of the dollar is significantly lower—and it's going to continue to drop. You need to account for that in your planning. Check out www.usinflationcalculator.com. One dollar in 1999 is worth $1.53 in 2019. Money needs to keep up, so we should aim to easily double our money over ten years if properly invested.

Second, there's planned obsolescence. Everything you buy is designed to break down eventually. If you have a house, eventually the roof will need to be replaced. You'll need to replace your washer and dryer. You'll need to repaint. Nothing lasts forever, so you have to plan to repair and replace just about everything you own.

Third, technology is constantly, and rapidly, evolving. Bulky, brick cell phones debuted in the '80s. The iPhone didn't appear until 2007. Then came the iPad and other tablet devices. Now we can see and answer the front door of our home from across the country with Ring technology. Alexa talks to you every morning when you wake up. What will we have tomorrow—ten years from now? Whatever it is, you know you will need (want) it.

These downward pressures are out of our control. We can't control what inflation is going to be. We don't know what is going to break down tomorrow and need repair or replacement. We don't know what technology is going to develop and make our current devices obsolete. We have no control over any of those economic factors.

Therefore, in order to live the lives we want, we have to build financial strategies that are able to adapt around these pressure points. For you to have any kind of life beyond just a roof over your head and food on your table, your plan should be able to adapt to beat inflation, to cover planned obsolescence, to keep up with technology. In order to win the game, you need investment models that are managed for these erosions.

Good Protection Means Controlling Your Controllables

Protecting yourself is not about building walls. It's about controlling your controllables. Good protection gives you the ability to move

> **Good protection gives you the ability to move and adapt.**

and adapt. If you get into a car accident, you have a plan. If you pass away prematurely, you have a plan. If you get sued, you know what is subject to creditors and what isn't. If you need to get money out of the market when it's down, you have uncorrelated money. When you need to retire, you know how much you can spend down. If the market is down when you retire, you know where you're going to pull from instead. For all the uncontrollable events that can happen in life, you can have safety mechanisms built in that adapt to those changes.

Protecting yourself sets up the game board so you can play the game on your terms—even when there are elements you can't control. It's about focusing on the other elements you *can* control. You can eliminate all your bad debt. You can control how much you spend on your house. You can say, "If I buy a house, my house payment will be under 25 percent of my gross income." You can control that. You don't want to become "house poor." You can control if you're a saver or not—and that's exactly what we'll be talking about in the next chapter!

CHAPTER SIX

BE A WORLD-CLASS SAVER

Before you can do anything else with your money, you have to save it. If you don't have any fuel, you can't go anywhere. You can't make money off your money unless you have that money saved. If you don't have any money saved, you can't use any of the strategies or philosophies we're discussing in this book. So the first step in using these philosophies and strategies to hack your financial future is to become a World-Class Saver.

Savings is simply money for delayed expenses. It's money for retirement, or should we say your new "work optional" life. It's money for planned obsolescence. You know, the things you buy that seem to break down right after the warranty expires, like a washing machine or refrigerator. It's money for technological change. We talked about the iPhone—now you need the iPad and Apple Watch, as well as a new iPhone at least every three years or your device won't keep up. New technology is always changing, and you will need it in the future. It's money for future taxes. It's good to live in the moment, but you also need to consider what your future is going to look like. Part of an abundance mentality is being future focused while also being in the present moment. Maintaining financial balance is about finding the balance between present and future.

> **Savings is simply money for delayed expenses.**

The Three Phases of Money

To become a World-Class Saver, it helps to understand the three phases of money: accumulation, distribution, and legacy.

Accumulation is exactly what it sounds like: it's when you're accumulating money. You go to high school, you go to college, and by the time you're in your thirties, you've started making some money. When you're in your forties, you're really starting to save and accumulate wealth. Your fifties and sixties are your peak earning years. That is all the accumulation phase, in the traditional sense. Ideally, we hack this and make it what you want. Like being work optional by forty-five!

Typically, somewhere between the ages of fifty-five and eighty-five, you start living off your life's work. Perhaps you've sold your business or you've stopped working, and now you have to live off your assets. This is the distribution phase, when you start using the money you built and saved during the accumulation phase. This is when you start converting the wealth you've accumulated into lifestyle, when all that life's work starts to come back to you as income.

Finally, there is the legacy phase: what happens to your money and assets after you pass away—what you leave to your family, what you leave to charity or other causes.

In order to build your wealth and let it provide for you in retirement, and still leave your life's work to the next generation, you want the three phases to be tied together. In a perfect financial strategy, you get the best of all three phases: achieving purposeful growth and accumulation; being able to spend and enjoy your wealth; and leaving wealth ideally to multiple generations after you.

Everyone's timeline for the three phases is different, depending on your *soul* purpose. For instance, for entrepreneurs and other Future Hackers, the accumulation phase continues even as they enter the distribution phase, because they are always growing and always building cash-flow investments.

Alternatively, the traditional model is built on a standard timeline: you work until you are sixty-five, you retire, then you die at eighty-five, having perfectly timed out your distribution so you've spent all your money. In plans built on this traditional structure, you save your money into an investment account, earning an assumed rate of return. By the time you retire at age sixty-five, you've accumulated a certain amount of money. Then, you are supposed to live on a safe withdrawal rate of 3 to 4 percent of your money, so you need to have enough accumulated that, at 3 to 4 percent, it generates enough income for you to live on. Then, if you pass away, the money in your principal would be divided in half, with half going to the government in estate taxes and the remainder left for the next generation. This is the perfect financial plan for the financial institution. Make money, spend only 3 percent, and let us hold it and invest in other companies so we can make a killing.

According to this traditional model, if you can live comfortably on 3 to 4 percent of the wealth you have accumulated, you are considered independently wealthy. This traditional advice that financial institutions offer—always keep your money invested, only spend 3 to 4 percent of it, and always keep it under management—sounds like good advice, but in reality, it promotes risk on the accumulation side. People struggle to get enough money in the pot to survive at 4 percent, and it encourages them to take shortcuts they believe will get them to that magic number more easily.

If given the choice between saving 5 percent of their income and earning 15 percent, or saving 15 percent of their income and earning a lower rate of return, most people are going to choose the former: putting the least amount of money in, with higher returns, to get them to that target of "independently wealthy." However, this strategy promotes financial risk. It puts you in an uncertain position. If the markets don't work out as planned, you may never make it. Guess what—the market never works out as planned. So it's basically all BS!

You don't know what's going to happen. You can't control the markets. Change is inevitable. The controllable in this situation is how much you save—understanding your downside and having a rules-based strategy you can stick with—and controlling that controllable is what makes you a world-class saver.

The Magic Number

Let's flip the model a bit. Accumulation is more than sticking money in a 401(k). It's taking control of your cash flow and putting 15, 20—even 30—percent of your money to work for you.

The average American only saves around 2 percent of their income. You should be setting aside a minimum of 15 percent of your income for future expenses—both long term and short term. For our clients, we even have a savings challenge of 30 percent.

Say you make $100,000 a year, so 15 percent of your income is $15,000. If you set aside 15 percent of your income over a thirty-year period, and you're earning a market-like return—say 7 percent—at the end of those thirty years, you should have $2 million. Then, when you retire, if that $2 million can earn 5 percent, it would pay you $100,000 a year—or, in other words, exactly what you were making in your working years. This is far more reliable than trying to reach the same place by saving 5 percent a year and taking on more risk.

What makes 15 percent the magic number? That's what's needed to cover all those downward pressures on your money as we discussed in the last chapter. We break it down like this:

Three percent is for keeping up with technology. Technology is advancing at crazy speeds. Even if you're not obsessed with always having the newest gadget, if you want to keep up with the modern world, you need to update your technology now and then. Plus, I can guarantee you that even if *you* don't, someone in your family is going to want the new iPhone.

Three percent is for planned obsolescence. Everything is designed to eventually break down. Your electronics, your appliances, your car. This is money set aside for those future expenses.

Three percent is for inflation. Think about what a Coke cost fifty years ago: six cents. Now it's $1.50. When your grandmother bought her house, she paid $20,000. Now, it's worth $2.5 million. Costs increase. This money helps cover the difference.

Three percent is for taxes—not just the taxes you pay every year, but to cover you if—or rather, when—taxes increase.

Finally, the last 3 percent is for lifestyle. This is money to live your life the way you want to live it.

Save before Everything Else!

Pay yourself first! Before you start spending money on anything else, you want to save this 15 percent. If you can't save 15 percent, you've got to figure out where your money is going. Is it going to unnecessary insurance? Is it going to taxes? Is it going to your debt? It could be due to the way you bought your house; perhaps you did a fifteen-year mortgage or you're accelerating the payments instead of paying it off slowly. It could be going to credit cards or student loans.

Even before you pay off that debt, you should save 15 percent. People think the first thing they should do with their money is pay down debt. But even if you have high credit-card debt or something of the kind, I'd rather you paid the minimum on your debt and save 15 percent of your income. Then you can figure out a strategic way to pay off your debt, bad debt first—in other words, pay off the debt that is not attached to appreciating or cash-flow-positive assets, any debt that has high interest rates, and any that's not tax-deductible. If you save, then you can accumulate your wealth and eventually pay off everything else easily. But you can't do that if you don't save first.

Another way to look at debt is to use the Cash Flow Index (CFI) method I learned from my good friend Garrett Gunderson, who is the founder at Wealth Factory and who wrote many *New York Times* best sellers. The CFI is simple: Cash Flow Index = Loan Balance / Minimum Monthly Payment.

The loan you should pay off first is the one with the lowest Cash Flow Index.

Inefficient Loans		Efficient Loan
Danger Zone	Caution Zone	Freedom Zone

0	50	100	300

Along with paying off debt, many people, as soon as they start making money, immediately upgrade their lifestyle instead of saving. Even though most people don't hit their prime income earning years until their forties, many tend to buy everything first and save last. As soon as they start making money, they go out and buy the big house, the nice car—and have nothing left to put away.

We have a financial residency program for physicians. Physicians are usually in school far longer than your average professional. They do four years of college, then get a higher-level medical degree, then do a residency, then do a fellowship, and then, finally, start practicing.

By the time most physicians get to residency, they're making around $50,000 a year. On that salary, trying to pay down an average of $200,000 of student loans, pay their bills, protect themselves, *and* set aside 15 percent is a challenge. So, many of them opt not to start saving. They think, "I'm not going to put myself in that situation, because one day I'm going to have a huge income and I'm not going to need money from now saved up."

The danger of this thinking is that once they start making more money, they haven't created the habit of saving. Instead, they start to increase their standard of living and still don't set anything aside. They don't systematize and standardize what they're doing.

Many doctors fall into this trap. Fast forward to when they're in their fifties, and all of a sudden, they realize their money isn't generating anything. They don't have savings that are growing. They aren't accumulating any wealth.

We would like those physicians making $50,000 a year to protect themselves for a million dollars, and start saving 15 percent—or $7,500—a year. How would they do that? By setting 15 percent aside every month, just like they would for any other bill. Then they can live off the difference. They were doing it before; they can do it now that they're making $50,000; and they'll be able to do it when they start making more money. The good habits formed when they are making $50,000 a year will continue when their salary rises—and their money will start to build on itself.

Successful people have good habits. Unsuccessful people don't. If you create those good habits now, they'll carry you forward for the rest of your life. I am where I am today because of the habits I started creating when I was just a kid. As a kid, I was always trying to set aside money for future expenses—and it saved my butt. Any time I made money, I'd put 50 percent of it away and have the other 50 percent for my future opportunities.

For years, my wife Laura saved 50 percent of her income. When we got out of school, we just set that money aside and let it compound in our whole-life cash-value insurance policies. When I got my first job, I thought, "Hell, I'm used to living on nothing. Why spend more money now?" I stayed in the same $500 apartment and had a $700 car. I saved as much as I could—and that's what allowed me to build what I have today. If I hadn't saved so much of my income, there's no way we could have created JarredBunch.

Create a habit of setting aside 15 percent by treating it as just another essential bill. If you don't pay your electricity bill, your electricity is going to get shut off. If you don't pay that 15 percent into your savings, your future will suffer. Think of it as a bill you're paying to yourself in the future.

One way to do this is to set up a separate account for future wealth creation that's outside your checking account—because we all know that once money is in your checking account, it's going to find another home! Instead, put that 15 percent into a new wealth creation account that is reserved for wealth-building purposes—and what you do with that account is what we will discuss in chapters 8 and 9.

It's Delayed Gratification, but It's Worth It!

There's no quick way to start saving, so it's essential to start early—because if you don't start early, it hurts.

You always hear wealthy people say, "The first million is the hardest." It's true: once you get a million bucks, the money starts accumulating faster and faster, thanks to compound interest.

> **There's no quick way to start saving, so it's essential to start early.**

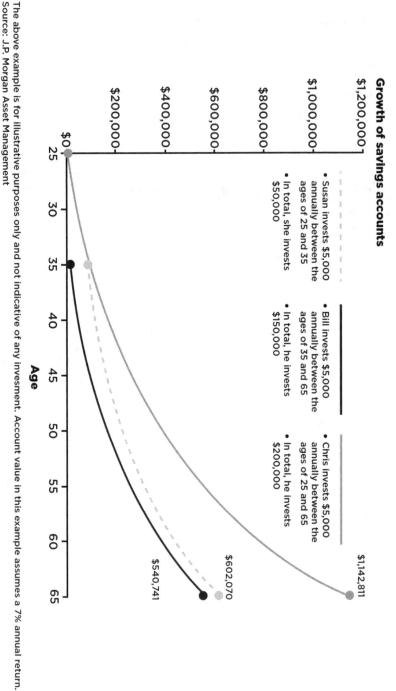

Growth of savings accounts

- Susan invests $5,000 annually between the ages of 25 and 35
- In total, she invests $50,000

- Bill invests $5,000 annually between the ages of 35 and 65
- In total, he invests $150,000

- Chris invests $5,000 annually between the ages of 25 and 65
- In total, he invests $200,000

$1,142,811

$602,070

$540,741

Age

The above example is for illustrative purposes only and not indicative of any investment. Account value in this example assumes a 7% annual return.
Source: J.P. Morgan Asset Management

Compounding refers to the process of earning return on principal plus the return that was earned earlier.

Say you make $100,000 a year, and you set aside 15 percent a year; you know that you will eventually have accumulated $2 million. That $2 million is your full wealth-building potential. But if you shorten the amount of time you're saving—say you wait to start setting aside that 15 percent until five or ten years later—the compound interest growth is cut almost in half.

The latter five years are where all your wealth is created. For instance, if you work for thirty years on a compound interest curve, you reach a million dollars around year twenty-five. The last five years is where it doubles to two million. Therefore, if you start saving five years late, either you'll never reach that last five years—or you'll have to work longer in order to reach it, or you'll have to save that much more. The longer you delay saving, the longer the hockey stick is. If you can start saving early, your compounding rate will be much higher in the future. The earlier you start, the better off you're going to be.

You can't short-change compound interest. It takes time to work. Of course, this can make it difficult, because you don't see the benefits immediately. You may be saving a hundred bucks, a thousand bucks, five thousand bucks a month, but you won't see great gains right away. Instead, you see the benefit fifteen, twenty, twenty-five years down the road. That's when compound interest really kicks in, and you start seeing exponential gains due to all the work you put in up front all those years ago.

It's human nature to want instant gratification. If we don't see an immediate benefit, it can be hard to feel like we're getting a benefit at all. When you pay off your mortgage, for example, you see an immediate effect. That's why it's often one of the first things people do when they start to make money. What they don't see is the long-term effects of locking up cash in an illiquid asset, instead of taking advantage of the lowest interest rate you'll ever get: the interest rate on a home mortgage.

Many people don't know what to do with their money when they start to make it, so they keep it in checking accounts, or they feel like they have to pay down their mortgage or pay off their other debt immediately. They don't put it where it can gain compound interest, so the compound interest curve never happens.

If your money is tied up in a house, you can't leverage it. If, instead of paying off your mortgage, you had saved that money and invested it appropriately over twenty years, you would experience the compound effect of that money and have exponentially more liquid money to spend. But people don't want to wait twenty years. They want the immediate gratification of paying off their mortgage now. There's an emotional benefit from paying off your home. But there's a great financial benefit from not paying it off early. You have to weigh the pros and cons for you. Any of our advisors can walk you through that process.

Saving Is Like Exercise— It Pays Off in the Long Run

Savings is delayed gratification—and humans, by nature, don't like delayed gratification. We want something that feels good right now, not later. In that way, saving is like exercising. You might not like it while you're doing it, but the payoff is totally worth it. You feel better, you're more energized, and in the long run, it'll help you live a longer and healthier life.

If you don't eat right, you get sluggish. If you don't exercise and get your endorphins flowing, you're not going to feel good. Then you start looking for artificial things to get you going, like sugar and bad food. And eventually, if you don't exercise, eat right, and take care of your body, something is going to break down—and then it will be harder to do everything else in your life. Taking care of your body extends to all the other areas of your life. It decreases stress and makes you feel better, which improves home life, improves your relationships, and makes you more productive at work.

The same is true with money. Living paycheck to paycheck is incredibly stressful. It's like running on a treadmill; you can never get ahead. Saving relieves that stress. You know that if something were to happen, you've got a cushion. Having that cushion gives you control. When you have control, stress levels decrease. When stress levels decrease, everything improves.

If you don't set aside money for yourself and take care of yourself first, then you won't be able to afford all the other things you need to do. Saving money saves everything else. If you have money in the bank, you can take advantage of new opportunities when they arrive. If a new job opportunity presents itself—like it did for me—you can take it, because you have the money saved to get you through the transition. If someone brings you a great investment opportunity, you have the cash to take advantage of it, creating a new stream of income.

Pay Yourself First

Many of the financial gurus of the world are so focused on paying down and eliminating debt that they undermine the importance of saving. We say, why don't you pay yourself first? Just like working out and eating right, the hardest thing to do is to set aside that money for yourself first. But insuring yourself first, protecting yourself first, paying yourself first—those are things you can control. None of our clients have ever regretted paying themselves first. The compounding and emotional effects are just too great.

And just as habit makes exercising easier, the more you can create a habit of saving, the easier it becomes to keep at it. It takes a disciplined effort to build that habit, but if you can do it, it will put you on the road to succeed. Then, you'll be in a position to hack your future by following the rest of the strategies in this book!

CHAPTER SEVEN

LIVE YOUR LIFE—AND INSURE IT RIGHT

I n a world full of uncertainty, three things are guaranteed: (1) life is constantly moving and changing; (2) you're going to die one day; and (3) you're sure as hell going to get taxed. Those are three things you can count on happening.

Now, imagine you could buy only one financial product to take you through a life in which only those three things are certain. What would be the financial characteristics of that product?

You'd want your money to be safe and guaranteed to never go away. You'd want it always to increase in value. You'd want it to be profitable, giving you a good rate of return—and once that profit is released, you'd want it never to be taken away. You'd want it to be tax-favorable, so you'd want it to grow tax-deferred. You'd want it to be protected from creditors. You'd want it to be protected if you ever got sued.

If you were to pass away prematurely, you'd want the company to pay out whatever your full future value is right now. If you live to a ripe old age, you want the value to keep increasing as you age, and you'd want it to all go to your beneficiary/beneficiaries tax free.

If you were to become disabled, you would want your future value to self-complete. You'd want it to be able to provide a lifetime income. If you need long-term care, you'd want to be able to access your money to cover those costs.

Finally, you'd want it to be a guaranteed lending source, from which you can always borrow money without applications or credit checks or other hurdles—rather than having to rely on banks, which are great at giving you money when you don't need it but terrible at giving you money when you do need it.

At JarredBunch we went through this exercise to figure out if a product this miraculous actually existed—and the result was absolutely astonishing. Most products—Roth IRAs, 401(k)s, straight stocks, bonds, or mutual funds—have their own benefits, but nowhere near as many as what we just described. You can't really take a big loan out of a 401(k); you can only borrow about $50,000, and you have to pay it back over a five-year period, which will put more pressure on your cash flow, and if you miss a payment you will be taxed. It might not be fully guaranteed. It for sure won't self-complete in the event of death or disability.

But one product that has been around for over two hundred years does exist and can do all these things: a traditional whole-life insurance policy backed by a participating mutual company—and it can be the heart of your financial plan if it's put together properly.

What Is Whole-Life Insurance?

Whole-life insurance policies have been around for centuries. Back when these insurance policies were invented, they were simply from a group of people putting their money into a pool of funds to protect their families if they should die. As that pool of money started growing, they said, "Let's put this money to work." The future profit was paid out in the form of dividends to the policyholders.

As the life insurance business started to grow, companies started to offer additional services—disability insurance, medical insurance, investments, annuities—and all these profit centers flowed into the company and provided profits to support the dividends as well.

In the 1980s, insurance companies were doing so well that many of them decided to go public—or, in other words, demutualize and cash out with an IPO (initial public offering). Instead of sharing all their profits with the policyholders in the form of dividends, they converted to stocks. As stock-based companies, they make a profit—but they are now looking out for the shareholders' best interests, rather than focusing solely on the policyholders.

To garner more profits for their shareholders, insurance companies created new products such as variable life insurance and universal life insurance. These are just new versions of a simple whole-life product that was created hundreds of years ago. That way, they could charge and transfer risk differently for the new products and compete against other companies' products, all while creating more profit for their shareholders. Whole-life policies didn't perform any more for these companies because they couldn't pay a competitive dividend as the company profits were flowing to the company stockholders, not the policyholders.

The companies that continue to be mutual have maintained

their original philosophy: their whole reason for existing is to protect their policyholders first and foremost, providing them with value and sharing all their profits with the policyholders.

Often, people look at all types of life insurance as being a cost instead of a living benefit, or something that adds value to you now and in the future. And it's true: while most insurance-based products—like auto insurance, medical insurance, and disability insurance—may protect you, they don't give you a return or benefit. A whole, or permanent, life insurance policy, on the other hand, has benefits far greater than just the death benefit after you pass away. In fact, you don't need to die to make use of the money. These policies can actually have real, tangible value while you're still alive.

The Problem with Temporary Insurance

There are two paths you can take when it comes to life insurance. Path A is to buy temporary term insurance and invest the difference. Path B is to buy permanent insurance and invest the cash.

Let's say you follow Path A. You buy term insurance that covers your $2 million in future value, to protect your value for your children should you die prematurely. You don't die prematurely, you live into retirement, you've achieved your $2 million in future value—and once that happens, that $2 million in term life insurance expires. It simply falls off the balance sheet. It will never be paid out. It's replaced by your $2 million asset, which will now go to your family when you die. So no need for that $2 million life insurance anymore, right?

Now you're sixty-five and retired, and you're going to start living off this pot of money you've worked so hard for. You've been making $100,000 a year your whole career, and you've done everything right—you've saved, you've protected yourself, nothing untoward like illness or disability has affected you—so you've now got $2 million saved. If that $2 million earns 5 percent a year, you would make $100,000 a year in retirement—so your retirement income would be the same as what you were making in your working years.

Of course, that $100,000 would be taxed—say at 35 percent. So, after paying taxes, you would receive $65,000 a year in income for the rest of your life—say from age sixty-five to age eighty-five, the average mortality rate. In total, over those twenty years, you would be paid around $1.3 million.

This is how most people retire. They would take home that $1.3 million from the interest and leave the $2 million to their family when they pass away. But this scenario assumes that you can get that 5 percent. What happens if you don't? Then you might have to dip into that $2 million. If you dip into the $2 million, then your interest goes down because your principal is lower.

Moreover, due to inflation, the purchasing power of $65,000 is going to decrease over those twenty years, as the price of goods and services rise. The future value of a dollar becomes less and less. Plus you have technology advancements, planned obsolescence, and those other downward pressures we've discussed. All of this puts pressure on you to earn not just 5 percent, but more than 5 percent in order to keep up.

Traditionally, advisors say that in order for your money to last, you should only be spending about 3 to 4 percent, so the 5 percent in this scenario is already kind of aggressive. And the more aggressive you get, the more risk you take on—just to survive on $65,000 a year.

That's why we like to approach things a little differently. We would like you to have exactly what you had before you retired. We would like you to be able to enjoy the wealth you've worked so hard to accumulate—and still be able to pass wealth on to the next generation.

Money has no value until it's applied to lifestyle. If you're living off only the interest and not actually putting any of your money toward living your life, what good is it? To have a life in retirement that is more than just survival—one where you can travel, spend time with your grandkids, give back to charity, mentor people, or whatever you're aspiring to do—you're going to need a surplus of capital. That's what you can have if you follow Path B.

Money has no value until it's applied to lifestyle.

WHY PERMANENT INSURANCE IS THE WAY TO GO

On Path B, you buy $2 million in whole-life insurance. When you retire, that insurance doesn't expire; it simply shifts from insuring your future value to insuring the $2 million asset that you have accumulated. Now you have your $2 million asset in your investment portfolio, *plus* the $2 million in life insurance coverage. Essentially, you are now worth $4 million.

This gives you a permission slip to enjoy your life's work. You can spend that $2 million dollars you've worked so hard to accumulate, because when you die, your life insurance policy will ensure that your family still receives a full $2 million dollars. Now, you have this $2 million earning you 5 percent, giving you $100,000 a year before taxes—but you no longer have to live on just $100,000 a year. Now you have that permission slip to take money out of your $2 million portfolio, because you know you have $2 million in insurance that will still go to your family.

Say you'd like to live on $150,000 a year. The first year, you take the $100,000 in interest you've earned, plus $50,000 from your portfolio. That means next year, you will make less in interest because your principal has gone down—but you'll also pay less in taxes because you're making less money. As you spend down your principal, you pay less and less in taxes, which then makes your income go up. If you continue this pattern, by the end of twenty years you will have spent nearly $3 million, rather than the $1.3 you would have spent if you'd lived on the interest alone—almost double the amount of income. And, you'll still be leaving $2 million to your family when you die.

The Traditional Way*
Person A

Year	Net Cash Flow	Legacy Value
1	$32,500	$1,000,000
2	$32,500	$1,000,000
3	$32,500	$1,000,000
4	$32,500	$1,000,000
17	$32,500	$1,000,000
18	$32,500	$1,000,000
19	$32,500	$1,000,000
20	$32,500	$1,000,000
TOTALS	$650,000	

Problems:
- Inflation
- Sequence of Returns Risk
- Disinvestment Risk
- Law of Large Losses
- Taxes

The Efficient Capital Management Way*
Person B

Year	Net Cash Flow	Legacy Value
1	$62,743	$1,969,757
2	$63,272	$1,938,002
3	$63,828	$1,904,659
4	$64,411	$1,869,649
17	$75,264	$1,218,507
18	$76,419	$1,149,189
19	$77,632	$1,076,405
20	$78,906	$999,982
TOTALS	$1,393,164	

Solutions:

- Increased Spendable Income
- Minimize Sequence of Return Risk
- Limit Disinvestment Risk
- Maintain Legacy
- Live Your Ideal Legacy

*This hypothetical Wealth Distribution Scenario is for illustrative purposes only. Net cash flow assumes the full basis for all assets. Other assumptions include a 20-year study period, $1,000,000 asset value, 5% rate of return and a 35% tax rate. This not meant to be construed as investment or legal advice. You should consult a professional concerning your circumstances.

Now, let's say you live longer than the allotted twenty years, and you've spent your $2 million asset. Well, you're covered for that, too, because you have money in your insurance policy. You can spend that money—or you could sell the policy. Say you're eighty-five and your life expectancy is another ten years or so. There are companies out there who would gladly give you a million bucks for your $2 million policy.

A whole-life insurance policy allows you to do more with less. It could allow you to retire earlier by allowing you to take more income. It could allow you to retire with less saved, because even if you only have a million dollars saved, it can spend like two if you insure it.

You can spend your total value—then leave your total value to the next generation. It's truly having your cake and eating it too. And don't you deserve to eat that cake? You've worked for all your life to make this money; don't you deserve to spend it? We think so.

We want you to be able to live your life and enjoy the wealth you've worked so hard to accumulate.

An abundance mindset says, "Live it up!" When you retire, you don't have to go out of use. You don't have to sit tight, trying not to spend any money. Instead, live it up! Spend every last one of your hard-earned pennies—and still pass down the same amount of money to your family when you pass away.

Permanent Life Insurance Doesn't Deserve the Bad Rap!

Permanent life insurance policies have garnered a bad rap because they are more expensive than term life insurance. Critics feel like they're not worth the cost, because they don't understand all the living benefits those policies can provide. If you understand how to use the strategy, insurance is not a cost; it actually creates wealth for you. Wade Pfau's article "Integrating Whole-Life Insurance into a Retirement Income Plan" is a very scientific look at whole-life insurance. Look at the science, look at the numbers, look at the facts, and it's pretty astonishing what you can do.

It's true that you do put more money into a permanent policy, because you are putting money into a contract that has a cash-value component. It gives you a rate of return. Term insurance, on the other hand, has a low monthly out-of-pocket cost—but you get nothing in return for it. Fewer than 1 percent of term insurance policies ever pay out, so it's very profitable for the insurance company but not profitable at all for you. You spend twenty years putting money into this policy, then it expires. That money you put into it is gone.

So why is term insurance so popular? Why is using permanent life insurance this way such a big secret? These policies are not widely discussed. You won't hear about them from the talking heads on TV. In fact, a lot of the talking heads will say, "Permanent life insurance is bad. Don't buy it." And yet they themselves often have these life insurance policies. Be aware, not all permanent life insurance policies are created equal. There are some bad policies and bad salespeople. The criteria we've discussed is the only type of policy that works the way we have explained it.

If you look behind the scenes, those talking heads are often sponsored by life insurance companies who want to promote term life insurance and investments. Do you think insurance companies really want to pay out death claims? Of course not! They make much more money on term life insurance, where they only have to pay out fewer than 1 percent of policies. Since they only have to pay out such a miniscule percent, term insurance is pretty much pure profit for insurance companies. No wonder it's what they market!

I say let's beat insurance companies at their own game. Let's create a plan to maximize your insurance. Let's set it up in a way where it will always pay out. Let's figure out a way for you to spend all your money. Let's hack your future!

The Secret Mix: Using Two Assets Together

Now, you may be thinking, "This sounds great, Scott, but how am I supposed to pay for this more expensive policy?" Well, if you think about it, by the time you're retired, you may have a combination of stocks and bonds anyway. If the policy becomes part of the bond equivalent and it grows like a bond, then it's just part of the allocation mix.

Say you got a traditional whole-life insurance policy with a good mutual participating company when you were in your thirties. You'd be looking at a thirty-year Internal Rate of Return (IRR) of around

5 percent on average.

"Well," you may say, "I've always done better than five in the market." Yes, that may be accurate. Most people know that insurance has a lower rate of return then the average of the stock market—but that's really only true if you look at it in isolation. So, let's say that you have a standard 60/40 portfolio: 60 percent stocks, 40 percent bonds. What's the thirty-year return on the bond? Five percent.

Your portfolio is designed this way to give you less risk—but bonds can drop in price too. Why not put something in there that has no correlation to the market, doesn't have that risk and volatility, *and* won't be taxable? Now the return doesn't feel like 5 percent; it feels like 7 percent, depending on your tax bracket. Then, what's the rate of return on the death benefit? It's normally around 10 to 15 percent *tax free at normal retirement age.* So now you have two rates of return working for you. That's why insurance actually could give you much more spendable money.

Instead of buying bonds directly in the market, you can put your money into a life insurance policy and protect yourself while *also* getting a risk-free return. Once again, it's using one dollar to do multiple things and accomplish the same result—or a better one, because now you have permission to enjoy your money.

Now, you have money in your portfolio—your equities and your investments, which we'll be talking about next chapter. And you have money that is protected against market volatility, increasing taxes, disability, dying too soon—all those things over which we have no control. It's the two working together that creates a great strategy. That's the secret!

This is an ideal financial situation. When you invest your money, you're usually put at risk. If you can protect yourself, use the money, and also invest, you'd have the best of both worlds—and that's what you can do with your policy. You can build your policy into your investment portfolio and still have a safe place to store cash and coverage.

This also allows you to access money without disinvesting. Disinvesting is when you pull money out of a portfolio while the market is down. When you disinvest, that money never has a chance to come back when the market goes up. If you had another bucket of cash that is stabilized and uncorrelated to the market, when the market is down, you can pull the money out of that bucket instead. Then, you can allow the money in your investments to come back when the market goes up again.

Instead of disinvesting, you can pull money out of a fixed, guaranteed, uncorrelated, secure insurance policy. When the market goes back up, you can pay back the policy. This protects the money in your investments. That's the power of using two assets coordinated to create a world-class strategy. The two things working together can both protect you and create more spendable wealth for you, while still leaving your money to the next generation.

A Guaranteed Lending Source

Pulling money out of your insurance policy as a guaranteed lending source can be a fantastic strategy—and one of the best examples of using the velocity of money.

Inside any life insurance contract, especially with a mutual life insurance company, there is a loan provision that allows you to borrow money against the policy at any time. Typically, you can borrow between 90 and 95 percent of the cash value of the policy. So, if you've got $100,000, you could borrow $90,000. In some cases, you can even get that money wired to you the next day!

When it comes to the interest rates on those loans, it varies from company to company. Some companies have annual fixed interest rates; some have variable rates. I've seen fixed rates as high as 8 percent, which is pretty common, but most strong mutual companies are now at 5, and variable rates as low as 4 percent.

Some companies will pay you the same dividend even though you have money borrowed out—in which case borrowing can even work in your favor. Say you're borrowing money at a 6 percent fixed rate and the dividends are paying you 6 percent. In that case, you're essentially not paying anything at all. And if the dividends are higher than the interest rate, you might be making money on the money you borrowed!

How does this work? Well, when you borrow money against your policy, you're not actually borrowing money from yourself or from the policy directly. You're borrowing from the insurance company. The actual money doesn't leave your policy. It's still there, earning dividends. So, even though the interest rate on the loan says 6 percent, when you factor in the dividends you're still earning, it evens out—or works in your favor. You can take out a loan, pay it back, and your policy hasn't lost any of its compounding interest.

This is what many sophisticated people do: they use their insurance policies as a good source of credit. They can use it to purchase other assets, get those assets to create revenue, get them profitable, and then pay themselves back.

When Walt Disney came up with his big idea for a fantasy theme park, everybody thought he was nuts. Not a bank in the world would lend him money. No Wall Street investors would touch the thing. But he knew his dream was worth building. He borrowed money on his life insurance money, and he built Disneyland. He was able to do this because he had a guaranteed loan. And given the success of Disneyland, I'm sure he made that money back and repaid his policy!

I've used this strategy myself: I bought my office building with an insurance loan. Once the building was cash-flow positive, I was able to get a bank loan, and I paid back my insurance policy. Now, I have both an office building that pays me rent, and I have the insurance policy still fully funded.

Think of how many assets you could acquire to create new passive streams of income—all while not impacting your compound interest, growth, and protection! There's no compromise. You can build wealth without losing anything.

Perhaps you decide not to do a 529 plan for your kid's college tuition and instead put that money into a life insurance policy. When your kid gets to college, you borrow money from the policy to pay the tuition. Now, say you also use that money to buy your son or daughter an apartment building that they can rent out to their friends. Income comes in from the rent, and four to six years down the road, you sell that building. You take all that income, and you pay back your policy completely, for the building *and* for the tuition. Now, you've basically sent your kid to college for free, because you've completely repaid yourself for the tuition!

You can also use a life insurance policy for what we call "the gift of a lifetime" for your kid. When your child is born, you can put in $10,000 for ten years into a life insurance policy for him or her. When he or she gets to college, you pull out $18 to $20,000 a year for college for four years. When they're ready to buy their first house, you pull out another $20,000 or $30,000 for a down payment on the house. Meanwhile, the policy keeps growing year after year. By the time they retire, they'll have a million dollars in the policy, and can get $50,000 a year of income. That's why we call it the gift of a lifetime!

Get Protected

Along with building wealth, whole-life insurance policies are also great at what they were originally built to do: protection.

When you buy a whole-life policy, you can add a disability rider to cover expenses in the event of a permanent disability. This ensures that, should you become disabled, the company will pay your premiums for you for the length of your contract, and still cover you for the same amount of your future worth, even if you are no longer able to work.

Remember my friend from chapter 5, who fell through a gap in his disability coverage when he got into an accident just before starting a new job? Luckily, he had a life insurance policy with a disability rider. The insurance company paid the premium to keep his insurance for his full future life value. He had been making a good income, so there was a decent amount of money in the policy. We were able to borrow money from the policy, buy some real estate to generate more revenue, then pay back the policy. The real estate now provides my friend with an income stream.

Because the company was paying the premiums, we could still borrow from the policy. Plus, we had included guaranteed insurability option riders, which meant that at certain stages he could exercise the option and buy more coverage, and the company would continue to pay the premium. So the money in his policy kept growing and growing.

Permanent life insurance policies also protect you from taxes. For starters, they have that cash-value component, which you can build by paying more than the scheduled premium and which will then grow tax-deferred. There is a limit on how much money you can put into your policy to grow tax-deferred, because back in the

1980s people were vastly overfunding their policies in order to take advantage of that tax-deferred growth. But for everything below that limit, there is a huge tax benefit.

That tax advantage doesn't just benefit you; it benefits your heirs as well. Because permanent life insurance is a death benefit, meant to go to your family and loved ones after you die, the money in the policy grows tax-deferred. Therefore, leaving your wealth to your family through life insurance is much better in terms of taxes.

Don't leave a taxable retirement account. Don't leave a big portfolio that will be taxed. Leave a tax-free life insurance benefit, and enjoy your money while you're alive.

A Swiss Army Knife

Most people have no idea that life insurance is capable of doing all these different things, because they don't fully understand it. And unfortunately, most advisors out there don't understand it either. They don't see the whole picture. Taken on its own, it's easy to see why some people think permanent life insurance policies aren't great. But when you look at how the policy interacts with all the other parts of your financial plan, it becomes a skeleton key that can open many doors.

A permanent life insurance policy isn't just a single tool. It's a Swiss Army knife.

A permanent life insurance policy isn't just a single tool. It's a Swiss Army knife. It's got everything. Whatever happens in your life, good or bad—whether it's an unexpected disadvantage you have to manage or an unexpected opportunity you want to seize—your life insurance can help you with it. It allows you to adapt to whatever comes your way. You just have to understand how to use it.

Many people misunderstand how to use a whole-life insurance policy because they look at it in a vacuum, not coordinating it with other assets. This is why it's so important to have a financial model that assembles all your information into a coherent whole, so you can look at all the elements together in one big picture. It's the combination of all these things working together to create a great financial strategy that allows you to hack your future.

CHAPTER EIGHT

BUILD YOUR GAME BOARD

I n the game of chess, each piece moves in a different way. The pawns move one square at time. Bishops move diagonally. Queens can move in all directions. Each piece has its own purpose and power—but it is nearly impossible to win the game unless you use all the pieces together in one coherent strategy. Sometimes you have to sacrifice your pieces to get an advantage at the end of the day. The best chess players use each piece for one common outcome: winning the game.

The same is true for financial planning. All the pieces need to work coherently together. When you are able to combine all your financial elements together to create a coherent strategy, you are building not just a financial plan, but a financial model that will allow you to adapt to nearly any move life throws at you.

This is where traditional financial planning has failed most people. The typical "planner" has likely been trained by a financial institution and asks a series of surface questions to move you into a single solution, product, or strategy that will "solve all your issues." I have been studying financial planning software and techniques for the last twenty years. It's amazing what's out there—wire houses can show Monte Carlo simulations of how you can asset allocate yourself to financial freedom by spending only 3 to 4 percent of your money; insurance salespeople will claim to be the "secret for your success" and try to show you how a simple annuity or life insurance policy strategy will be your "saving grace" when everything falls apart on you. Then there are infomercials showing how you can get rich quick in a variety of ways. I've tried nearly everything and researched all of them: there is no quick solution to anything.

We hear this story over and over again from people who become our clients. Very rarely have I seen a company addressing your whole financial life with a "model" that incorporates all life contingencies—now through the three stages of money accumulation, distribution, and preservation.

What Is a Financial Model?

Traditional financial planning is based on a set of assumptions. You have a certain dollar amount, a certain time period, a certain savings amount, and a certain interest rate you're going to get on each dollar. Is it really that simple? Can you take a static linear approach to see where you will be twenty, thirty, fifty years from now? What happens if you lose your job, get into a car accident, get sick, or have to take care of a loved one? What happens if the market doesn't perform, the cost of living increases much faster, you quit your job to start a business? That's why financial plans are nearly impossible to set. They forget that, as people, we are always evolving and changing.

A financial model acknowledges that we don't know what life will throw at us, but we do know where we want to go and what kind of life we want to live. We know what the big picture looks like, but we don't know what all the obstacles will be, what journeys we'll take, what will hit us along the way.

A model looks at your present position and situation and makes sure you are financially balanced and optimized to take on these obstacles. Part of that is making sure you are organized and protected for your human life value. You've paid yourself first and set aside a minimum of 15 percent of your total income for wealth-building purposes. You've eliminated bad debt. You have a rules-based system for making financial decisions. You know that you are going to hit hurdles and roadblocks along the way, but being optimally balanced gives you the ability to react to those changes. Having a rules-based model, a systemized way of looking at things, allows you to stay nimble and adaptable enough to adjust to what life throws at you.

The Big Problem: Failure to Communicate

Unfortunately, there's often a big disconnect between all these different pieces of people's financial plans. Say you have an advisor who works for an investment company. Although they present themselves as a wealth advisor, their primary responsibility is to manage money. They're typically not looking at the whole picture or using comprehensive financial models to weigh and measure financial decisions and how they impact one another. On the other hand, if your advisor is a life insurance agent, they'll be well-versed on the protection side—but they may miss the wealth management piece.

And even if you have both advisors, they're probably not communicating with each other. They're each working only on pieces of the plan, and there's no coherent comprehensive strategy. They each may not have all the information. They each may have a certain way they do business. They each may have a different belief system. They each focus on their microspecialty, but at the end of the day, how does it all connect? When they weigh and measure decisions, typically they aren't basing decisions on a cohesive financial model they both share. When you don't have a rules-based system and a financial model, it's difficult to capture lost opportunities. It's difficult to find lost money and put it back to work. The advisors can't use velocity-of-money concepts or make money do two or three things, because they don't have all the information in front of them. They only have bits and pieces.

The Comprehensive Approach

We look at everything comprehensively, holistically. We build financial life models. To do this, we break everything down into four financial dimensions—some of which we've already discussed in previous chapters: protection, assets, liabilities. And cash flow.

Assets are where your money is stored. Your money might be stored in investments. It might be in a business. It might be in real estate. It might be in personal property. There are all different kinds of assets. The money you have in savings is also an asset, as is the money you have in what are called nonqualified accounts, like stocks, bonds, and mutual funds. Qualified accounts are ones from which you can't easily pull out money and then put it back in, such as IRAs and 401(k)s, and those are assets as well.

Your cash flow, as the name implies, is the inflow of cash to you. This could be a salary, bonus, dividends, rental income, interest, business distributions, etc. When you are working, you make a certain amount of money. When you make it, where do you put it? Do you pay down debt? Do you use it to buy more assets—personal property, houses, savings, investments, retirement, a business? Where does it go?

Many people don't really think through where their money goes. Typically, we find that around 3 to 5 percent of people's money is just leaking out of their pockets, going to high insurance costs, debt, taxes, or a variety of other things. If we can recapture that money, we've gotten you a 3 to 5 percent return just on cash for the rest of your life. Now, if we put that money to work, even if it got a modest 6 to 7 percent, **we've now compounded that money for the rest of your life**. One dollar saved today could be worth six times that thirty years from now. That can make a dramatic impact on your financial future.

You also need to consider how much money to keep liquid for emergencies. Through our years of experience, we've come to the conclusion that our clients should have a year of liquidity before they start tying up money, before they start paying down debt, before they start putting money into retirement accounts from which they can't withdraw it, before they do anything that will cause them to lose immediate control of their money.

At the very least, you should have enough money to cover three to six months of expenses liquid, so if you have any issues—whether you lose your job or have a temporary disability or an unexpected cost arises—you have a buffer. But ideally, you have a whole year of liquidity available—enough money to get you through an entire year—before you start tying up capital.

You should also check your financial vitals the same way a doctor checks your physical vitals at a checkup. Make sure you're maintaining that 15 percent going to savings. Make sure you have no bad debt. Make sure you have three to six months—or even better, a year—liquidity.

When those vitals are in place, then you can move to the next cornerstone of your financial model: investment.

Your Investment Philosophy Is the Rule Book for What You Do with Your Money

As Warren Buffett says, "If you don't find a way to make money while you sleep, you will work until you die." If you don't put your money to work, it has a return of zero. If you just set it aside into a savings or checking account, if you don't invest it, it won't earn any money. It has no possibility of earning anything. Why does this matter? Because of all those eroding pressures on your money we've discussed: inflation, technological development, planned obsolescence, taxes. Because of this erosion, you're actually losing money every day your money sits there doing nothing.

> **If you don't put your money to work, it has a return of zero.**

Anyone who wants to really hack their future needs to have an investment philosophy for the money that is put to work. It doesn't matter what pieces you have; if you don't have a game board to put them on and rules to play by, you're never going to win the game.

If you look at any person who has been incredibly successful with their money, you can usually break what they've done down into four or five basic rules and tenets they used to succeed. They did something along the way that allowed them to survive when adversity hit, when most other people were wiped out. It wasn't luck; it was having a strategy and rules they could adhere to.

Investments are supposed to be inflation-adjusted hedges. We don't want you speculating or gambling. We want to set you up with money that's protected, so you can use it to take advantage of these opportunities when they present themselves. It's all about positioning yourself for that time to allow you to take advantage of the next opportunity.

In 2007 and 2008, if you had properly adjusted your portfolio for downside risk protection, you could have taken the money you protected from the massive market correction and used it to buy nearly any asset for next to nothing. That's what smart money does. It's the same thing the Rockefellers did in the Great Depression—they were positioned well and bought up everything they could. They were able to do this because they had money ready, so they were able to seize the opportunity.

There were people who speculated, shorted the market in 2008 and 2009, and came out on top; but those people have not had luck trying to repeat their success. The people who had rules-based philosophical systems with evidence behind them have fared much better.

You can't be your own bank without having an investment philosophy. You can't use the velocity-of-money concept until you have an investment philosophy. You can't gain enough money to buy more real estate, finance deals, or grow a new business if you don't have a smart management strategy.

In the stock market, you only make money when you sell. Even if you bought at the right time, unless you sell at the right time too, you won't make any money. Often, people buy stock, and if it drops way down, they can't handle it anymore, and they sell it, instead of waiting for it to go back up—which it almost inevitably does. But without a philosophy to stick to and rules to abide by, their emotions take over, they get too nervous that it'll never go up, and they just want to get rid of it.

Having a Philosophy Protects against Emotion

After all, money is deeply emotional. It's your livelihood—literally what keeps you alive. It's tied to the deepest instinctual, emotional drives within us. Because of this, it can be very hard to stay strong. This is why average investors don't do well. According to Dalbar's 2018 Quantitative Analysis of Investor Behavior study, the average equity investor earns only about 4 percent. The reason for this, according to the study, is because they make decisions based on emotions. When you don't have a philosophy you can adhere to, emotional behavior takes over. You think, The market's too high; I need to get out! Or, The market's too low. I can't handle it; I need to sell! Our emotions take hold, and we don't make decisions based on actual evidence. As the following chart shows, investors are taken on an emotional rollercoaster as the market moves up and down. The stock market is the only place where customers most typically buy when the price is high and sell when the price is low. This emotional roller coaster is the primary driver for that behavior. And the results are disastrous.

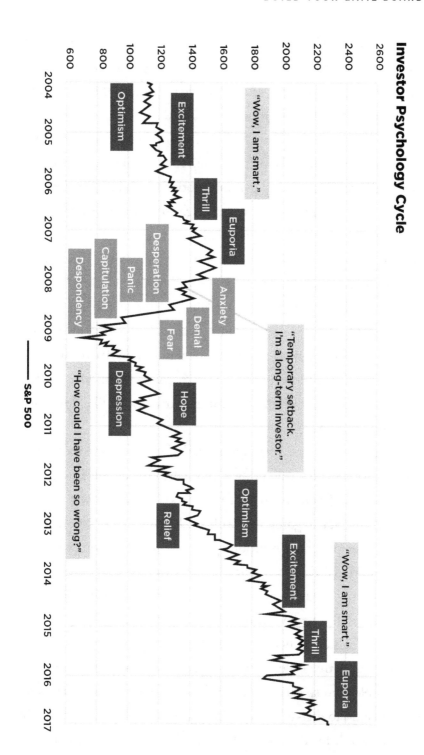

Source: Real Investment Advice

Unfortunately, many financial advisors can be just as bad as the clients when it comes to making decisions based on emotion rather than evidence. The truth is, the smarter you are, the more you're going to trust your intuition and make decisions based on a "gut instinct." This usually leads you to do something that puts you in more trouble, rather than helping you. The factual piece goes out the door, and you start trusting your emotions to make the decisions, because you figure you are smart enough to beat the system.

Popular culture is always telling romanticized stories about winning based on instinct, on choosing from the gut. But real life is more like the 2011 movie *Moneyball*, which is itself based on real life. In the movie (and in real life), Oakland Athletics general manager Billy Beane used evidence, facts, logic, and math to build a winning team, defying conventional wisdom. What really works, Beane found, is following the evidence, following the facts. That's what will allow you to build a winning portfolio, just like Beane built his winning team.

I can also tell you what *doesn't* work. You can't time the market. It's very hard to pick when to get in or when to get out. Fast picking rarely works. If you try to beat the market on your own, and you get it wrong, you're going to get off track really quick. Not adhering to any principle-based solutions puts you in a position where you make emotional decisions, and that gets you in trouble. Occasionally, following a gut instinct pays off, but almost inevitably, it only works once. The people who have done well from gut instincts get one swing right, but then they keep missing. By the time you average that one hit with all the misses, they come out on the losing end.

People who speculate and gamble with their money, who stock pick, who try to market time, typically put themselves in more trouble than it's worth for the potential reward. This creates more emotional stress, which then prompts them to make more emotional decisions. It becomes a cycle of anxiety, fear, and depression. People are afraid they don't have enough money, so they make poor, rash decisions to try to catch themselves back up. Those moves often result in having even less money. Then they try it all over again. It's an endless, self-perpetuating cycle. In gambling terms this is called being on tilt. Annie Duke explains this in her book, *Thinking in Bets*, where an investor has a bad result or has anxiety that causes them to be "on tilt," which leads to making (usually) overly aggressive decisions to make up for the tilt. The consequence almost always is an even worse result.

The best way we've found to break this cycle is to help our clients create for themselves an investment philosophy, a policy statement that truly works for them. You have to find some form of evidence, some strategy you can adhere to, rather than speculating and gambling with your money. You have to have a rules-based system behind it to help you hold your behaviors in check, a system you can stick to through thick and thin, one you can live with.

When things change and you get nervous or frightened—which is the natural human reaction to change—you have rules to play by so you don't make an impulsive decision and don't go on tilt. And it's not just having rules to abide by when things go badly; it's also having rules to abide by when something is really exciting. It's easy to get sucked in by the next shiny thing that comes along, like many people have done with Bitcoin. The rules make you ask, "What's the evidence behind it?" Early adoption is usually just speculation and gambling.

This strategy will be more important than the actual money itself, because now you have the rules to the game. You can deal with what's going on. You have protection mechanisms and alternative options for when things don't work out as planned. Having an evidence-based strategy, rather than a theory-based strategy, increases the chance of success because it uses data, not emotion, for investment decisions. A systematic, rules-based philosophy eliminates human bias and costs, giving you a smoother investment ride that helps you stay on track.

Keeping It Simple and Transparent

We work to create these strategies not just for you, but *with* you. We want you to understand the strategy completely. We want it to make sense. That's why the rules we create are simple and transparent. If we make a trade, we say, "This is why we made this trade. This is the rule behind the strategy that informed that decision." You know going in what we are likely to do. You understand exactly why we're doing what we're doing with your money.

We have a client whose brother is with a different firm. "I asked my brother what he's doing with his portfolio," our client told us, "and he said, 'Well, my advisor must be pretty smart, because every time I leave a meeting with him, I have no idea what he said. I just have to trust that he knows what he's doing, because he seems pretty smart.' But he has no idea what's going on with his own money."

To us, that's a major issue—and yet that's how many advisors operate and how many people feel about investing. Many people don't seek out the advice of an advisor because they feel like they're going to be sold something or they feel like they're not going to understand or they feel like they're going to be talked down to. "These people are way too smart," people think. "I'm not going to understand it, so I'm going to have to blindly trust them, and I'm going to end up getting screwed over because I won't know what they're doing. I don't want that to happen, so I'm just going to do it myself. I'll just follow my gut." They don't have any strategy. They don't have any rules to follow. They might talk about it with their buddies at work or watch financial talk shows on TV, but chances are both will just give them bad advice or misinformation.

Alternatively, many other people think, "It's too over my head. I can't deal with it. I just have to blindly trust somebody else." Unfortunately, that "somebody else" all too often doesn't necessarily have your best interest in mind, because they're a registered representative and are limited to the solutions of whatever company they work for.

In some cases, standard brokerage firms and the like want to push the products they've created and use those in your portfolio. It could be alternative investments. It could be credit-default swaps, derivatives, active trading, etc. You might get these funky types of investments that are really just some new fad the company is using to try to build a portfolio, rather than using an evidence-based strategy. Our experience (and research) shows that simplicity trumps complexity. Transparency trumps "black box."

Transparency and simplicity help you avoid the inherent biases and incentives built into many advisors' investment philosophies. The advisor who considers himself a market timer is going to trade often, which will incur many trading costs for which his client will pay him. There are also the proprietary or commission-based mutual funds, which advisors will buy under the guise of diversification, or even under the guise of modern portfolio theory, but are really just a way for advisors to make money on the commission they get from that fund.

When we were stuck in the broker-dealer world, we had to represent the broker-dealer. We didn't represent the client. In that world, it was nearly impossible to have an evidence-based-philosophy conversation with a client, because the broker-dealer didn't offer all the options. We could only offer the products the broker-dealer offered.

Now we have access to every strategy we want, and we never ask anyone to blindly follow us. We'll make sure you understand what we're doing. We've got your back. And we're working in your best interest. We're open about how we charge, how we invest, how we create our portfolios, how we rebalance. Everything is very simply laid out, then put into a software system that organizes, executes, and controls your investment philosophy.

> **You shouldn't have to live in ignorance or fear, making decisions based on emotion.**

You don't have to have a PhD in finance to understand it. You just need to understand the rules and say, "I like these rules. These are the rules I want to stick to." Then you can understand exactly what you're doing with your money, even if you don't have any financial education at all. You shouldn't have to live in ignorance or fear, making decisions based on emotion. We want to help you pick the investment philosophy that works for *you*. We want you to be able to invest confidently. It's your money, after all!

134

CHAPTER NINE

CREATE AN EVIDENCE-BASED INVESTMENT PHILOSOPHY THAT WORKS FOR YOU

S everal years ago, after the Great Recession, I went to our chief investment officer and asked, "How are we going to protect our clients during the next recession?" We had made adjustments to our strategies during the rough time, but there were no set guidelines or rules for why we made the changes. I feared that our investment strategies weren't as good as they should be at avoiding large drawdowns in the market. This began the journey of looking at hundreds of strategies that have been used by investors. He and I began studying, researching, and modeling scores of investment philosophies, theories, and strategies. We challenged our own deep-seated beliefs, including the most prevalently marketed modern portfolio theory.

What we found shocked us!

First, almost all the strategies we studied work. So, it's really hard to be wrong … with some key caveats:

Time frame is critical—many rely on thirty, forty, fifty-plus years to be successful.

Human behavior is the biggest failure—a strategy must be maintained over time to be successful. Frequent changes undermine success.

Diversification helps but can create problems if "too" diversified.

Most ignore two key issues: sequence-of-return risk and longevity risk.

Investors must suffer through drawdowns to achieve returns.

The Popular Strategies

The first of the most popular strategies I learned about was modern portfolio theory (MPT). MPT, created by Harry Markowitz in 1952, is at the foundation of evidence-based investment philosophy. Markowitz basically said, "Here's the evidence: stocks and bonds have a correlation. This is how we can harness that correlation." Today, nearly all strategically managed investment accounts are based on this tenet.

MPT involves taking a series of assets—for instance, stocks and bonds—and mixing them together so you get a good rate of return with lower risk and volatility relative to the stock market. Stocks typically have more risk and return than bonds, which gives them a higher standard deviation and market volatility than bonds. Typically when stocks are performing well, bonds lag. When stocks are doing poorly, bonds do well. You mix them together, and you have a correlation that will allow the portfolio to keep moving in the right direction of the market with lower volatility.

Another strategy is the Fama-French (FF) Three Factor Model we discussed in chapter 4. The Three Factor Model essentially says that factors such as business size (small versus large) and value have better returns over time. When you get a better return for small and value, you naturally have more risk. Using MPT in combination with FF, you can take your risk out on low-duration bonds, which have really low risk versus longer durations bonds and which add more small and value stocks and equity to your portfolio.

In our research project, every strategy has to have its own rules. In MPT, you're periodically rebalancing your portfolio regardless of what the market may be doing. In the FF Three Factor Model, a certain percentage is held in factors that give you a better return, and you take less risk in bonds, since you can make more on equities over time. That's the way portfolios are constructed following that model.

These are the backbones of traditional buy and hold strategies espoused by 95-plus percent of investment advisors. There's nothing wrong, per se, in these philosophies, but see the caveats stated earlier.

Creating a Comprehensive Plan

We actually don't believe that following any one of these strategies is the best and only investment philosophy. Strategies like MPT and the FF model are not wrong; they're just incomplete and easiest to execute. For example, some firms believe purely in modern portfolio theory, so they have a computer program which generates an allocation based on that algorithm, rather than having an investment advisor provide input on the selection beyond a basic risk-tolerance profile. In this instance, when the allocation is selected by a preset MPT program, it becomes overallocated and overdiversified among many different asset classes, without one asset that is really generating meaningful output. There are many holes in MPT, and even Markowitz himself didn't follow it. But we won't get into all those details in this book.

Pure MPT also misses two big key elements in the market: sequence-of-return risk and longevity risk. The theory works fine as long as you have fifty to one hundred years to invest. Over that amount of time, the market generally goes up. If you step back and look at the overall picture of the market from its birth until now, the line goes up. From that perspective, it's simple to say, "I should invest in the market for diversification, because the market always goes up."

But when you step closer to the picture, you start to see all the nooks and crannies. You see the volatility, the drawdowns, the periods of loss. You see that in some downturns it takes a decade just to get back to zero. Now, imagine if you had retired during that downturn; you might not have a decade to recover. Imagine if you had to pay for your child's college education during that time period or if you had become disabled and needed to use that money. MPT doesn't address those life changes. MPT says, "Hold on forever, eventually the market will go up." But that's not how life works.

The other theories have similar gaps. So, rather than adhering to one single strategy, we believe in creating a network of strategies that create a comprehensive evidence-based philosophy.

We look at all the evidence-based strategies. We look at MPT. We look at the FF models. We look at the Ivy League portfolio and the Yale endowment. We look at the All Weather Portfolio of Ray

Dalio—one of the best investment managers of all time— which he created in order to manage his own trust. We've studied scores of investment strategies and mapped them out: the maximum drawdowns, the highest returns, the volatility of every given portfolio, etc. From that we've created our own investment strategies based on the evidence from our research.

So when we meet with a client, we go through our findings and help them create an investment philosophy for themselves. We also believe in setting specific goals for each bucket of money. Your one-year liquidity bucket has one agenda, because you need to be able to access that money at any time. Your retirement accounts have a different agenda, growing tax-deferred or tax-deductible. Since each bucket of money has a different agenda, it therefore has a different strategy. Each part of your portfolio has different rules associated with it. All those strategies and agendas come together to create the big-picture financial plan.

People ask, "What's my risk tolerance?" In traditional financial planning, a risk-tolerance assessment is taken, and that risk tolerance is applied across the entire financial plan. Our answer is that your risk tolerance is different for each bucket. The risk tolerance on the money you need to buy a house is different than the risk tolerance on the money in your retirement account, which is different than the risk tolerance you need on money to send your kid to college, which is different than the risk tolerance on the money you've set aside to start a business. The risk tolerance varies based on where the money needs to be set aside to achieve a specific goal.

We believe that an evidence-based philosophy should be created for each separate bucket of money. Each element of your financial life adheres to its own philosophy, and they all come together to create a comprehensive financial model.

Finding the Strategy That's Right for You

Most of our clients, when they come to us, already have money invested. So, we start by looking at what they are currently doing. What is the risk of that given portfolio relative to the market? What other strategies could they be using? What would those look like? We walk our clients through the different options, comparing risk, returns, results.

Rarely does someone come into our office who has everything set up right. They have no rules-based system for their investment strategy. They have no evidence-backed reasoning behind their decisions. They're speculating, trying to grow by gambling with their portfolio dollars. And yet they don't spend any energy on protecting themselves. They say, "I can't spend money on that because I have lost opportunity to build over here." And yet when they are trying to build money, they're not doing it with any kind of rules or evidence-based system.

However, just because you've been doing one thing with your money up until now, or because you haven't had a strategy up until now, doesn't mean it's too late to get started or to change to a new, evidence-backed strategy.

So, how do you find what evidence-backed strategy is right for you? Everyone is uniquely different. The investment philosophy that works for me isn't necessarily going to be the investment philosophy that works for you. Everyone's goals are different, their timeline is different, their life events are different, their perspectives are different. How do we address these unique differences? How do you decide what evidence-based strategy is right for you, what philosophy you will be able to adhere to?

Looking at each investment strategy backed by evidence, you should ask, "What's my risk? What's my volatility?" You have to understand what the risk of doing business is, what the real return opportunity looks like, and how you can adapt and move a portfolio through changing economic conditions. If you pick life insurance, for instance, you'll have no risk. It doesn't go down. But, since it mostly gets a bond-like return, it also doesn't outpace inflation by that much, and it should allow you to take more opportunistic risk with your other money.

What your friend is doing that works super well for him might not work for you. He may be happy to weather extreme ups and downs; you may be happier with a smoother ride. Whatever the reason is, you need a strategy built for you.

A smoother ride also helps your portfolio's growth potential. For instance, say you had $100,000 to invest and you lost 50 percent of your money in the first day and the next day you gained 50 percent. Your IRR is 0 percent, but you lost 25 percent of your money. How did this happen? Well, 50 percent of $50,000 is $25,000 so money and math are two totally different things. The compound growth of a dollar has much more pressure with large drawdowns. The higher the volatility, the less ability your dollar has for compound growth over time. So, our goal is to minimize large drawdowns and to smooth out volatility as much as we can in order to get greater compound growth within a portfolio. We can't avoid volatility, we can't avoid risk, we can't avoid drawdowns, but we can minimize and/or control them to some degree to provide a smoother investment ride for the client. This not only helps compound their dollars over time; it also makes it easier to stick with their strategy!

Emotional and irrational decisions are usually made during large drawdowns. If we avoid large drawdowns, you won't find yourself in those emotionally fraught situations, when you are more inclined to make irrational, emotion-based decisions. In my example about someone losing 50 percent in the first day, it's highly unlikely that the investor will hold on to get back to even.

The Most Effective Strategy Is the One You Can Stick With

Of all the strategies out there, we've found the most effective one is the one you can stick with, the one you can hold all the way through. They say the best exercise is the one you can stick with. They say the best diet is the one you can stick with. We say the best financial strategy is the one you can stick with.

Sometimes, people pick a strategy they think is right for them and then discover that, in fact, it doesn't work for them at all. Maybe they thought they could handle the risk, but in practice they find they're not comfortable with it. Maybe the strategy is not giving them enough growth. We see this all the time, and when it happens, we go back and reeducate the person on the options and help them select a strategy that they will be better able to adhere to.

However, we also see a lot of people who, when the market's doing well, say, "I want to get more results!" and want to change their strategy. Then when the market's doing poorly, they say, "I don't like this!" and want to change their strategy again. Remember, a strategy only works if you stick to it. If you want to change it every time the market changes, based on what you are feeling, you're once again falling into those emotional behavioral patterns. Changing your strategy based on emotion is the same as making investment decisions based on emotion.

Staying the course is what pays off.

Staying the course is what pays off. Warren Buffett proved this in 2008, when he bet the hedge fund industry $1 million that they could not assemble a portfolio of hedge funds that would beat the returns of one Index Fund, the S&P 500, over a ten-year period. Sure enough, by the end of the ten years, the S&P gained 125.8 percent, while the hedge funds gained only around 36 percent.

Pick the strategy that is right for you and then stick with it. Don't let emotion convince you to change it. Continually changing your mind can be incredibly detrimental. If the market drops, the worst thing you can do is change your strategy. You need an investment strategy you can stick with, based on a form of evidence that really works for you based on your particular situation.

Of course, you can't pretend emotion doesn't exist. People are going to feel excited when the market goes up. They're going to feel scared when the market goes down. To counter these feelings, we bring our clients back to the underlying reasons they chose that strategy in the first place. We remind them what is important to them, what they set out to do, so they can stick with it through all the ups and downs.

If, after everything, they do want to change strategy, then we make sure they understand both what the upside is and what the risk of loss could be. We make sure they have all the information and all of the evidence, so they can make the best decision possible.

What an Evidence-Based Philosophy Can Do

Once you are completely confident in your evidence-based philosophy, you can sign off, saying, "This is my investment philosophy statement. This is how I want my money managed." Once you do that, we as a firm will abide by those rules and make sure your portfolio follows that philosophy.

When you've decided on an evidence-based philosophy that works for you, you can use that philosophy to guide all your future investments. This saves you from making investment decisions based on emotion or gut instinct.

It also ensures that your money will continue working for the next generation. Most endowments, trusts, pension plans, and other large assets that are passed down have an investment policy statement that sets out the rules on how the money is supposed to be managed. If you're leaving money to your family, you can help them out by making it easy for them and showing them how to make the money work. All you need is the simple parameters an evidence-backed investment philosophy provides. Then, you just have to say, "It's got to fit these parameters."

An evidence-backed philosophy also gives you an expectation of what the drawdown could look like, what the returns will look like, what the results will be. Anytime you put money in the market, you're going to have volatility. There's no way around it. Ideally, we could manage our money without risk at all and only have gain. But investing results in risk. If you don't take on any risk, you're not going to get a very good return.

What's important is having a level of expectation of what that risk and volatility will look and feel like for your portfolio—which you can do by looking at the evidence behind the strategy you've chosen. How did it work in past market cycles? If that market cycle repeats itself, you wouldn't get exactly the same results, but you'll have an idea of what the volatility would look like.

Because it's backed by evidence, it's much easier to understand how a given portfolio reacts to something. When you know the evidence behind it, you can understand the behavior. You understand what ups and downs are normal and how things will work themselves out over time. That makes it much less scary and stressful.

Of course, it's well known that past performance is no indication of future performance. You can't invest based just on track records. You can't invest based on what did well last year, because those could be the worst performers this year—and in fact, they often are. However, a good evidence-based strategy is built to adapt to those changes, to however the world is moving—and not just in the marketplace.

You can't predict the future. What you can do is see how a given strategy reacted to something that's happened in the past. The past may repeat itself in some way or form. You can look at the history and say, how would it work in a higher-interest-rate environment? How would it work in a war? How would it work in a debt crisis? How would it work if the Republicans take over? If the Democrats take over? Your entire financial plan needs to be able to evolve—and your investment philosophy needs to as well.

Picking a strategy and sticking to it doesn't mean going rigid and inflexible. It sounds counterintuitive, but in fact, picking a strategy and sticking to it is what gives you the ability to adapt when things change. These strategies are not iron cages. They're not things you set in place and then walk away and do nothing. They simply provide the rules to play by so you can stay on top of and win the ever-evolving game. They are designed for change.

Having a strategy prepares you for change by giving you the rules so you know what to do when change happens. A strategy allows you to adapt your portfolio to change based on the evidence behind the strategy. When you have a philosophy to stick to, you don't have to worry about making emotional decisions. You don't have to agonize about what you feel is the "right" thing to do. You have evidence-based rules to guide you.

The best investment strategies don't only prepare you for change; they harness the power of change. For us, we employ strategies born out of our research—the evidence that uses the factors that have proven performance over time with methodologies shown to reduce risk and drawdowns.

CHAPTER TEN

GET SOME MOMENTUM WITH FACTOR VI

I nvestment theory is constantly evolving. Back in the 1950s, Harry Markowitz created modern portfolio theory, saying if you have stocks and you have bonds and if you mix them together correctly, over a very long period of time, you can have a result similar to the stock market with less risk. This was the birth of the diversified portfolio. MPT had its place back then, and many advisors use it today. The concept of diversification is good, especially when you have very long time horizons. MPT uses expected returns and correlations to create a portfolio. Unfortunately, expected returns are projections into the future and rarely hold true. Same with correlations.

In the 1980s, the Fama-French (Ken Fama and Eugene

French) Three Factor Model was developed. They discovered that equities outperformed fixed income, small cap stocks outperformed large cap, and value outperformed growth. They later introduced a fourth factor, quality, and then a fifth, profitability. While this model largely holds true today, we've seen long periods of underperformance for both value and small cap companies.

Ray Dalio and Jim Rogers were big commodities traders who showed us what adding uncorrelated asset to a portfolio could do—both positive and negative. The evolution continues with quant investors like Meb Faber, Gary Antonacci, Alpha Architects, Resolve, and Newfound. These managers are creating and publishing new research, rules, and evidence for investing.

As you can see, the investing is an evolution based on uncovered evidence, changing market dynamics, changing technology, and greater access to new information. The one constant has been sentiment. People generally have acted irrationally since the beginning of time, and there's no indication that will ever change. Markets have a tendency to rise and fall with sentiment (emotion) as well as the other factors we've discussed.

Fama and French discovered momentum all those years ago. They called it the persistent anomaly. They didn't know what to make of it. Many managers still don't know, even though they may speak of it. Momentum is the underlying current of the market.

Our philosophy is to harness momentum in combination with the other factors to create a strategy to accomplish three goals: reduce large drawdowns, minimize volatility, and produce strong returns over time. For example, we noted before that there have been periods where small cap has underperformed large cap. Using momentum (trend following) as a factor, we would have exited small cap when it began to underperform and switched to large cap.

Every factor has a rule associated with it so there's no guesswork or market timing but a defined entry/exit criteria. The simple example below shows a trend-following criteria (two-hundred-day moving average) to either be invested in the S&P 500 or not. Over time this method reduces large drawdowns, minimizes volatility, and produces strong returns.

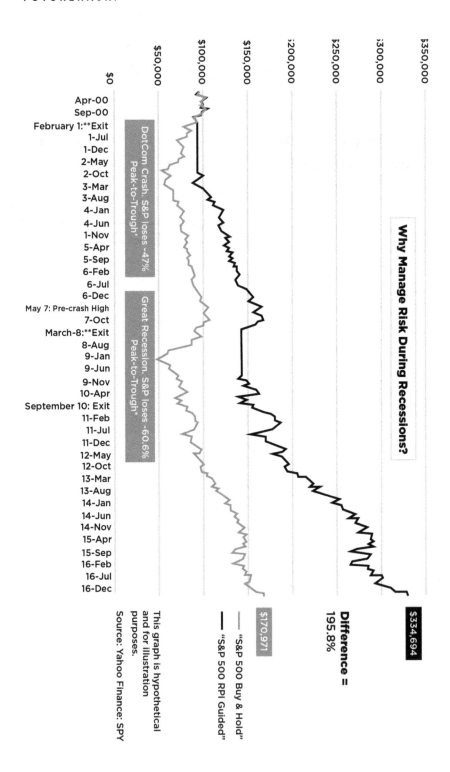

Why Manage Risk During Recessions?

DotCom Crash, S&P loses ~47% Peak-to-Trough*

Great Recession, S&P loses -60.6% Peak-to-Trough*

$334,694

Difference = 195.8%

$170,971

"S&P 500 Buy & Hold"

"S&P 500 RPI Guided"

This graph is hypothetical and for illustration purposes.

Source: Yahoo Finance: SPY

Momentum becomes the ultimate hack for investing. Like all investment strategies, it has its downfalls. Sometimes you get whipsawed, where an asset class looks like it's trending when it's not. So you buy high and sell low. Or the market fakes you out. Like in 2018, when there were three straight down months followed by the largest January gain in eighty-seven years. Almost any investment strategy will work. If you stick with it and give it enough time. Our research shows that momentum is the best factor to help you address both. Legal speak here—past performance is no indication of future performance. Your performance will vary.

How to Harness the Power of Momentum

The secret sauce really is that there is no secret sauce. The best investment strategy is the one you can stick with through good times and especially through bad. You'll experience both many times over throughout your life. It's the combination of factors we've already mentioned combined with momentum (trend following) that we feel gives you the best opportunity for winning.

The one constant factor impacting the market has been momentum. Trends are clearly seen throughout the history of the market. Within those trends there are certain companies, industries, sectors, services, products, etc. that thrive and others that would not. Identifying these trends and the areas receiving the most

> **The one constant factor impacting the market has been momentum.**

benefit is the nature of trend following. Using a defined set of rules and criteria, removing emotion and guesswork from making decisions, is the hallmark of a good momentum strategy.

The figure below shows emotional responses to events and perceived events and the movement of the market as a result. This is just a ten-year period.

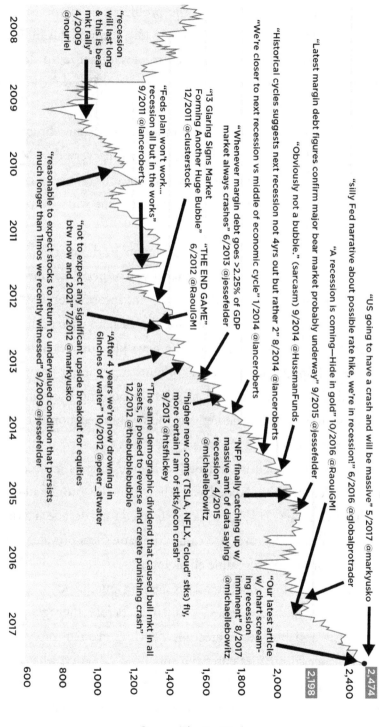

Source: The Fat Pitch

The world is ever changing. The proliferation of the internet has created an overload of information. Sadly, most of this information is false. The headlines are written to sensationalize, to draw in readers/viewers often without regard for the facts. And we've become a headline economy making decisions based on the headline versus the underlying story. This leads to emotional decisions. Emotional decisions are often bad ones. We see it play out every day. Money managers, institutions, pension funds—no one is immune. Sentiment drives markets. Therefore we believe momentum will always be a pervasive factor.

What else creates trends and movements in the market? Information is a big one. It used to be that if you've heard the news, it's too late. The market has already priced it in. Information moves so quickly now (especially false information) that markets tend to react quicker. This can be good and bad. Big news like changes in interest rates always impacts the market. Economic news about unemployment, industrial production, retail sales, or housing starts impacts different segments of the market. We follow these economic indicators as they come out. And these are just a few.

Certain factors fall in and out of favor. Value as an example. Warren Buffett has been lauded as the best value investor of all time. Yet value, as an asset class, has underperformed for a decade at a time. This wasn't always the case. Are value companies less prevalent or is the criteria for identifying value changing?

Rapidly growing small firms are getting purchased by private equity or large publicly traded companies before they go public themselves. Arguably, this is creating a decline in small cap growth rates. As fewer companies enter the small cap category, what is the impact on the ones already there? The change in this asset class could have a ripple effect on the future of outperformance or underperformance of the asset class. The Fama-French modeling of the past may not be as solid as it once was. Only time will tell. Trend following allows us to make moves and benefit, without having to make that bigger decision.

Our society is evolving and changing rapidly. Cultural shifts are happening. Marijuana is now legal in many states. Sports gambling is now legal. Even new digital currencies are being introduced. Technology is advanced. Social norms are changing. New businesses and opportunities are being created. Ten years ago the iPhone didn't exist. What new technology will change our lives ten years from now?

Follow the Trends with Evidence

There are plenty of ways to invest. Our experience is there are several that just don't work. Or at least don't work over an extended period of time. For example, stock picking is a typical way people invest. There's a company I like or I heard about. So I buy it in my brokerage account. Sometimes the value of the stock goes up and sometimes the stock goes down. The average person loses when they try to pick winners. Typically, and this is supported by data, investors buy stocks that are hot (have increased in value a lot) and sell when they go down (have dropped in value a lot). You have to be right twice: when you get in and when you get out. Investing is known as the only industry where most people buy when prices are high and sell when stocks go "on sale." Sure, your best friend made a killing on the stock he told you about. But he didn't tell you about the others he lost on, or he's not telling you the truth and he lost his a$$. Stock picking can be a short-term boon, but ultimately it is a long-term loser for most people. I see many online retail brokerage accounts with many positions with a loss as they sold the winners and are stuck with the losers.

Speculating and gambling in the market doesn't work either. Many of those looking for a big win, a home run, and a way to make up lost ground turn to this method of investing. They speculate on which digital coin will be more popular, like Bitcoin or Ethereum; they speculate on which marijuana stock will take over the market. They speculate on whatever they think is going to be the next big thing. If they're right, great. But if they're wrong, they end up causing themselves major harm.

If you are going to use a momentum-based strategy, you better have rules, otherwise you will just be speculating or gambling, market timing or stock picking. Following trends is not the same as market timing. Market timing is guesswork, and nearly impossible to capture. It may be an educated guess, but it's still a guess. You'll hear people who are trying to time the market say, "The market is too high; I need to get out." Or "The market is so bad that there's no way it won't go back up soon, so I'm going to wait to buy." But you can't predict the future.

Evidence-based investing uses a defined set of rules, criteria by which you buy and sell. While you can do this with individual stocks, momentum works best, in our experience, with asset classes and/or index funds. For instance, in the US, Morningstar identifies eleven distinct sectors into which the stock market is divided: energy, financial services, healthcare, real estate, telecom, technology, raw materials, industrials, consumer staples, utilities, and consumer discretionary (which includes retailers, media companies, apparel companies, etc.). Stocks are also designated into categories, such as large cap, large value, small cap, small value, international large, international small, and international value (and more)—those are all defined asset classes. When it comes to bonds, you have short-term bonds, intermediate-term bonds, long-term bonds, and such—all verified asset classes.

These asset classes are represented by ETF's (exchange traded funds) or mutual funds. They are traded easily with strong enough volume that you have liquidity to get out as needed. Thinly traded assets, without much volume, can be harder to trade.

Use Momentum to Manage Volatility

Using momentum (trend following) is also a way of managing volatility. Most people are more familiar with the traditional way of managing volatility: balancing stocks and bonds. In 2007 and 2008, when the market corrected, if you were 100 percent in stocks you might have lost around 55 percent, because the market dropped that dramatically. If you had 50 percent in stocks and 50 percent in bonds, you would only have dropped 27 percent—much better. Many investors' main issue is they don't want volatility, so they will only be a fifty-fifty investor and will never be able to capture the full upside of the market. However, if you had used momentum, you would have noticed when the market started to trend positive or negative, and you could have moved into a different mix or equity/fixed income allocation. As the equities market trended negatively in 2007/08, a momentum strategy may have increased your allocation to fixed income. Thereby you have missed the biggest portion of the drawdown. As the market trended back up in 2009, you may have reentered to capture more of the upside. This is the nature of trend following.

When we back tested all the evidence-based strategies for managing money, we found that momentum-based, trend-following strategies experienced lower volatility, reduced drawdowns, and offered a similar ability to participate in the upside.

Of course, it is essential to be protected from large drawdowns. Why? Because math and money are two different things. Say you put $100,000 into a given portfolio. If you lose 50 percent, you'll have $50,000 in that portfolio. If you gain 50 percent the next day, your rate of return will be zero, not negative—after all, you lost 50 percent and gained 50 percent, which equals zero. However, the actual amount of money you have will only be $75,000, because 50 percent of $50,000 is $25,000.

Although math says the rate of return is zero, the money says that you lost 25 percent of your cash to those volatility gremlins. The math makes it look like everything's in good order, but in reality, the volatility gremlins are eating away at your portfolio, which will impact what you have to enjoy, spend, and live on. This situation is even worse when you're in retirement and you need to pull out money when you're down that 50 percent. If you pull that money out while you're down, it will never have a chance to come back. That's the disinvestment problem we discussed. You're disinvesting versus reinvesting.

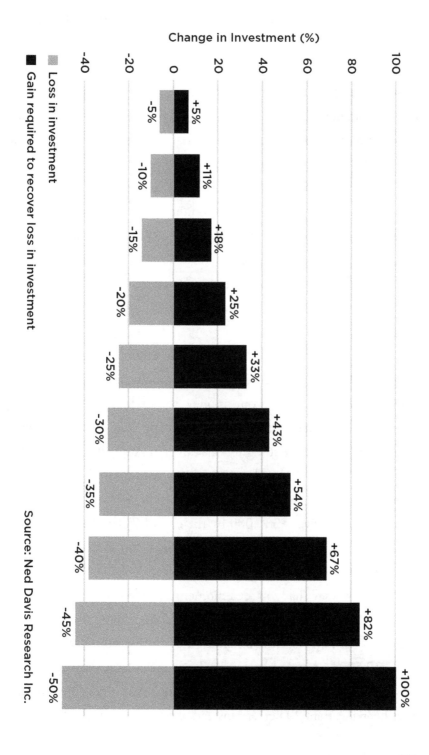

Change in Investment (%)

■ Loss in investment

■ Gain required to recover loss in investment

Source: Ned Davis Research Inc.

Momentum offers you a buffer from downside risk while keeping you invested with an evidence, rules-based approach to exiting losers early and riding winners. There's no need to just "ride it out" through large market drawdowns. If the market's on a bull run and stocks are going up, then we'll tilt that way and hold the assets that are trending in that direction versus the ones that aren't. If stocks are going down, we'll move into something with less risk.

We do this by establishing a system of rules, where certain movements in the market trigger certain actions. For example, you could say, "I'm going to own large cap stocks over a long period of time, but once the market moves below its ten-month moving average and starts to turn negative, I'm going to move to cash or fixed income position." Now, you've created a rule, a trigger, based on momentum.

For example, say that you invested $100,000 in the S&P 500. From 1999 to 2018, the S&P 500 has grown nearly 283 percent. That's good—you want your money to double every ten years. However, it also had some large drawdowns. Just a year after you invested, you had three straight years down in 2001, 2002, and 2003. Then, in 2008, the index dropped 55 percent and took 883 days to recover. All told, if you kept your money in the S&P the whole time, you would have over $380,000 by the end of 2019. But could you, did you, just wait it out? Most people didn't and sold at the wrong time, then entered back in at the wrong time.

Now, let's say that you set a momentum rule: "When the market trends below the ten-month moving average (or something similar), there's a shift to treasuries. When it goes positive, you invest back to the S&P 500." This simple strategy helps avoid large drawdowns. In this hypothetical back-tested example, your max drawdown would have been less than 20 percent instead of 55. By limiting volatility on just one index, one S&P 500 ETF, your upside changes substantially. Instead of generating 283 percent, it could have generated over 660 percent return.

By putting just one variable on there, momentum, you could have ended up with $750,000 instead of $380,000. How? Because you're able to minimize the volatility/drawdown during the 55 percent drawdown. So, when you put your money back into the S&P when it starts moving up again, you're stepping off at a higher point. You don't have to recapture all the money you lost, because you never lost it. You've had a smoother ride, *and* your money grew by a much greater percent—just by applying that one factor. Legal speak again: this is a hypothetical example. Past performance is no guarantee of future performance. Your results may vary.

Our Secret Sauce

Unfortunately, the rules of financial institutions can limit the ability to build these strategies. Most retail institutions have their own models. Some may even use a momentum-based strategy. There are hundreds if not thousands of flavors of momentum. We keep ours very simple and transparent. They've got their own way of doing things. And often, they don't have the compliance structures or technology in place to execute those strategies even if they did allow them. So there aren't many people talking about these kinds of strategies, because the big institutions typically don't have the ability or desire to build or execute them for retail clients.

Where you do see these strategies, apart from small fiduciary firms like ours, is in the larger institutional money managers or family offices. You don't see them in the big commission-based companies. The majority of advisors—and therefore clients—simply don't have access to strategies like these. Personally, I have yet to see any strategies like our Factor VI Strategies offered in a retail setting. I have seen articles written about them; I've seen academic papers, but I haven't seen anyone building these strategies as a product for the typical consumer.

Because of this, using momentum to build trend-following investment strategies is unique to us. The secret sauce is the combination of multiple factors in our strategies. One thing doesn't work by itself; what makes it successful is unifying the factors and having them work together.

We created Factor VI Strategies to reduce drawdown and provide downside risk protection; to decrease overall volatility, creating a smoother investment ride; to allow investors to be in equities longer; to put investors in a defensive market position when needed; and to eliminate reliance on timing or being in during a certain time period to capture growth.

The strategies we built are created from a diverse set of robust factors proven to work: size, value, and momentum. The combination of how we use these factors is our "secret sauce"—implemented in a completely transparent manner. While they are simple to execute, they are also extremely well-researched and real-world tested with our own clients and with other investment managers.

Momentum Needs a Solid Foundation

In order to really take advantage of momentum, you need to have in place everything else we've discussed in this book. You need to protect yourself, find your lost money, stay organized, have an evidence-based investment philosophy, use velocity-of-money concepts, and understand the rules of financial institutions. You need to make sure you're adaptable to change—because momentum is about riding change. You have to pick your strategy and stick to your rules. You have to follow the evidence. You have to be an abundant thinker, always evolving to be better. You have to understand the rules of financial institutions, where to use them, and more importantly how they limit you. You have to control your controllables.

When you combine all these elements together, then you can truly harness the power of momentum (and a true financial model) to hack your future and reach your full financial potential.

CONCLUSION

IT'S TIME TO #FUTUREHACK!

N ow that you've gotten to the conclusion of this book, I'd like to ask you to do something. It's going to sound a little strange, but I promise, it's worth it.

I'd like you to write your obituary, as it would read if you died tomorrow. Write down all the things you've done and accomplished. Put it all down on paper. Now, read it over. Did you do everything you wanted? Is your life complete? Did you spend as much time with your kids as you wanted to? Did you make time for your spouse? Did you give back to charity? Did you go on that trip you always wanted to go on? Did you start that business you always dreamed about? What have you left unsaid? What have you left undone?

Now, take another piece of paper, and imagine that you could extend your life for as long as you want, longer than humanly possible, if you'd like. Now, write your obituary as it would read if you died after that long, long life. What would it say? What are all the things you would like to have done in your long life? What are the top ten things you'd want to accomplish now that you have all the time in the world? What are all the things you're going to do? Take that trip? Start that business? Go back to school? Be work optional at fifty and spend more time with your family? What do you want people to say about you? What do you want your kids to say, your spouse, your business partners, your employees, your friends, the people who are most dear to you? How do you want to be defined? What is your legacy going to be?

Why did I ask you to do this? Because that second obituary—that's your story. That's your *why*—that's your Future Hack. We live our lives day to day, without ever really sitting down and thinking about the big picture. Life moves fast. Things are always happening. Often, we can't see the forest for the trees. The obituary exercise is a little bit morbid, sure—but it gets your mind out of the day to day and into the big picture of what you want your life to look like, what you want your future to be.

For each one of those things you write down, you can start to strategize, focus, and identify the key characteristics that will help you get there. What are all the reasons you think you can't do something? Why can't you go on a trip? Why can't you start that business? Why can't you become independently wealthy at forty? Identify each of the objections, each of the reasons why something "can't" happen.

Then, approach each of those *can'ts* from a mindset of abundance. Use them as the raw material for the solution. Start creating a plan around each one of those objections. Now, you have action items—

small, accomplishable lists of the things you need to do to reach your big goals. By the time you go through this step-by-step process, you'll find that you have the foundation of a game plan for living the life you want to live. You'll be living in a world of abundance, instead of a world of scarcity, a world of "can't."

We're here to help you with the financial aspect of reaching those goals. That's why the question we start with isn't, What does your ideal financial future look like? The question is, What do you want your life to look like? Like we said in the beginning of this book, money means nothing. It's what you do with the money that matters. That's the foundation of your financial plan. You get to write that story; we're going to help you live it. We can help you build a financial road map to ensure you're living the life you really want to live in a world of abundance where you're not afraid of change.

> **You get to write that story; we're going to help you live it.**

* * *

If you truly want to live in an abundant, always evolving world, you have to create a system in which you put your money to work. You have to understand the velocity of money. You have to understand the basics of how money works with inflation, with planned obsolescence and technological changes. You have to know that it's okay for the haters to hate, and that the more successful you get, the more hate you're going to get, and that's cool. More money, more problems, as they say. You have to bring all the elements we've discussed in this book into play.

While the world is ever changing, the elements we've covered in this book, the elements you need to create a financial strategy that allows you to reach your full financial potential remain the same. You still need evidence behind your investment strategy, as well as rules that make sense. You still need to be protected for your value. You still need to be adaptable; you still need to evolve. You still need to control your controllables. There will always be people who have an agenda for your money that's not in your best interest whether they are aware of it or not. There will always be people who live in a scarcity mindset. And there will always be the option to live in a world of abundance.

The world changes and evolves. Even this book will continue to evolve. But these elements don't. These hacks are forever.

In order to truly use these hacks, you have to dig deep and really know what you want your future to be. You can't do any of this unless you know where you want to go. You have to ask yourself the tough questions, because nobody else is going to ask them of you. It's not my financial plan; it's yours. It's not my future, it's yours. It's not my story, it's yours—and only you can tell it.

What we can do is help guide you on that journey, creating an executable financial strategy to make it happen. That's your road map. This is something most financial planners don't offer: a road map based on your ideal future. Most financial plans are built on need, asking only, What do you need? We're in the wants business. What do you want? What is possible? And how will your financial strategy help you get there?

At JarredBunch, we want to help you discover how to live out your why. We want to help you identify what's possible. We want to help you live in abundance. We want to help you hack your future.

That's why we start with your mind first—having an abundance mindset, always evolving, not letting the haters derail you. Then, we make sure that you can adapt to change, that you are protected, that you are controlling the things you can control, including saving and insuring yourself properly. Finally, we make sure you have an investment plan you can really get behind, backed by evidence, with rules that you can follow to keep you on the path toward your ideal future.

We start with the big picture, and as we get closer and closer to that future on the horizon, things start coming more into focus. The abstractness becomes real, and your strategy becomes a reality.

A Call to Action

I know it can be hard to make that first move. So many people are afraid of financial planning. They're worried they've been doing things wrong, or they are just too busy. They're anxious about their future. It's a difficult, very personal conversation.

I want to assure you that when you arrive at JarredBunch, you enter the judgment-free zone. The first thing we say is, "Don't worry about where you've been in the past. Just think about where you're going. We're just going to show you where you currently are and help you discover where you want to go. We're going to discover opportunities. We're going to identify your bigger future. We're going to hack your future."

The first step in this process isn't figuring out where you want your money. The first step is figuring out what you actually want, figuring out your why. We want to get you thinking about what's possible before we even get to the numbers. From there, we back into everything else. With every new client, we go through this discovery process to start identifying your why, what your money is for. That's more important than the money itself. That's where the journey starts.

Then, we want to get an understanding of what your current

position is. To do this, we have a simple subscription fee that pulls and integrates all your financial data and helps you identify your most important objectives.

One of the main ways we help our clients through this journey is by becoming your personal Future Hacker, like a financial coach and personal CFO, helping you to realize your bigger future. That's our service. Instead of saying, "Here's a plan that will cost you this much money," we want to empower you to take and expand this journey yourself. We want to help you organize yourself in an effective way to help you weigh and measure the pros and cons of every financial decision you make. We want to give you the tools and resources necessary to make your future better and brighter than ever. We'll guide you, but we want to put the power in your hands to make decisions for yourself.

Once we get you set up the right way and put that power in your hands, we don't disappear. At any time, we can plug in and help you. At any time, we can help you navigate your next steps. But you are the one in control. If we can protect you in all these areas without any additional out-of-pocket cost, if we can enable you to hit your future growth goals and do everything you want to do, if we can empower you to reach your full financial potential, then we have done our job.

There's no reason to wait. If you want to start this journey, if you want to make these changes now, if you want to start hacking your future today, then we're just a phone call or a click away, at 1-855-288-5588 or www.invst.com. Now's the time to #FutureHACK your life!

APPENDIX

INTERACTIVE FUTURE HACKS

In addition to working with us as guides to build your financial plan, you can also engage with us through one of our innovative interactive Future Hacks, all of which can be found on our website, www.invst.com:

InvstIQ

InvstIQ is financial interval training, much like HIIT (high-intensity interval training). In fitness, HIIT is one of the most effective ways to exercise. The same is true for your financial well-being: one of the most effective ways to reach your full financial potential is through financial interval training.

Your financial life consists of four phases, or intervals: Reveal, Protect, Grow, and Sustain. These are the building blocks of your financial life. Each one is essential and can't survive without the support of the one before.

InvstIQ takes you through each of these four intervals, giving you valuable resources that not only teach you how to successfully conquer that interval but also help you apply what you've learned to your life. InvstIQ takes you through some of our financial planning process on a do-it-yourself basis, allowing you to move through the modules at your own pace, without an advisor.

WealthBuilder

WealthBuilder is a digital platform tailor-made to house the important financial data from all parts of your life. Using state-of-the-art calculators and data integration, WealthBuilder provides a real-time view of your financial life. You can now easily weigh and measure financial decisions by stress testing your financial model. WealthBuilder turns data and information into effective action. It gives you the power to put your complex financial life into one organized dashboard. It gives you one point of coordination for cash flow, investments, savings, and more and allows you to measure the impact of your decisions before you make them. By doing this, WealthBuilder empowers you to make every decision a smart one.

Invest with Invst

You get one shot at this financial journey. You'll have opportunities for success and even greater opportunities for failure. But failure is not an option when you work with us. Our strategies are built with this in mind. They put downside protection first to create a smoother investment ride and keep you disciplined over the long term so you can reach your full financial potential. Sophisticated wealth management strategies used to be reserved for only the wealthiest investors; now we're offering them to everyone.

CPSIA information can be obtained
at www.ICGtesting.com
Printed in the USA
JSHW020300041121
20125JS00001B/3

9 781735 111209